For your readi

LONDON'S

STRANGEST TALES

THE THAMES

Other titles in the STRANGEST series

The Ashes' Strangest Moments
Boxing's Strangest Moments
Bridge's Strangest Hands
Cinema's Strangest Moments
Classical Music's Strangest Concerts
Cricket's Strangest Moments
Fishing's Strangest Days
Flying's Strangest Moments
Football's Strangest Matches
Gambling's Strangest Moments
Golf's Strangest Rounds
Horse-racing's Strangest Races
Kent's Strangest Tales
Law's Strangest Cases
London's Strangest Tales
Medicine's Strangest Cases
The Military's Strangest Campaigns
Motor-racing's Strangest Races
The Olympics' Strangest Moments
Poker's Strangest Hands
Politics' Strangest Characters
Railways' Strangest Journeys
Rock 'n' Roll's Strangest Moments
Royalty's Strangest Characters
Rugby's Strangest Matches
Sailing's Strangest Moments
Science's Strangest Inventions
Shooting's Strangest Days
Television's Strangest Moments
Tennis's Strangest Matches
Theatre's Strangest Acts
World Cup's Strangest Moments

LONDON'S

STRANGEST TALES

THE THAMES

EXTRAORDINARY BUT TRUE STORIES

First published in the United Kingdom in 2014 by

Portico Books
10 Southcombe Street
London
W14 0RA

An imprint of Pavilion Books Group Ltd

ISBN 9781909396487

A CIP catalogue record for this book is available from the British Library.

10 9 8 7 6 5 4 3 2 1

Printed and bound by 1010 Printing International Ltd, China

This book can be ordered direct from the publisher at

www.anovabooks.com

Cover image ©Science Museum/Science & Society Picture Library

CONTENTS

The Saxons Find God, AD 635   12
London Bridge Falls Down, 1091   14
Matilda's Frozen Flit, 1142   16
Avian Arithmetic, c. 1150   18
A Not So Deadly Duel, 1163   20
A Polar Interloper, 1252   22
The Rout at Radcot, 1387   24
Beasts of the Thames, 1457   26
The Big Chill, 1608   28
The Underwater King, 1620   30
A Rose by Any Other Name, c. 1644   32
The Famous Trout, 1670s   34
Badge of Honour, 1715   36
A Very Royal Musical, 1717   38
The Bridge with No Excise, 1769   40
Felons Afloat, 1776   42
The Punctual Shark, 1787   45
Thames Flows the Wrong Way, 1792   47
The River Beat, 1798   49
Grand Designs, 1802   51
Nelson's Final Journey, 1806   53
Boat Race Starts with a Bang, 1829   55
The Killer River, 1858   57
The Two Alices, 1862   59
The Fear of Floods, 1868   61
Going Underground, 1876   63
Too Close to Call, 1877   65
The Agony of the *Albion*, 1898   67
Celebrity Island, 1912   69
The Sub That Didn't Sink, 1918   71
Crossing the Divide, 1926   73

Water, Water, Everywhere, 1928   75
Life in the Saddle, 1933   77
The Great Crab Grab, 1935   79
Going the Extra Fourteen Miles, 1937   81
Amy's Mysterious Demise, 1941   83
A Ticking Time Bomb, 1944   86
The Mystery Monster, 1956   88
Winston's Final Farewell, 1965   90
A Little Piece of America, 1965   92
A River Holiday, 1967   94
The Phantom Hitchhiker, 1972   96
Father Figure, 1974   98
Anarchy Aboard the *Queen Elizabeth*, 1977   100
Dockers Threaten Disaster,1982   102
Shuttle Service, 1983   104
Prescott's Political Protest, 1983   106
Winnie's Legacy, 1984   108
Letter from Beyond the Grave, 1999   110
Wheel of Misfortune, 1999   112
The Real Brain Drain, 2001   114
Dive, Dive, Dive!, 2001   116
Fowl Play, 2001   117
Hicks' Heroics, 2001   119
Fayed Funny Backfires, 2002   121
The Lifeboat Delivery, 2002   123
Papering over the Cracks, 2003   125
You Can Lead a Horse to Water, 2004   127
Malcolm's Marvellous Marathon, 2004   129
You Cannot Be Serious, 2004   131
A Dramatic Spark, 2005   133
White Water, 2005   135
Pharaoh Floats By, 2007   137
A Long Journey's End, 2007   139
Doggy Paddle, 2007   141
Rugby Replaced by Rowing, 2007   143
One Hell of a Wels, 2008   145
Diving for Treasure, 2008   147

A Manacled Demise, 2009   149
Tale of the Tape, 2009   151
Water Wings, 2011   153
Fisherman's Nasty Bite, 2010   155
Record-Breaking Regatta, 2012   157
Muddy Waters, 2012   159
Room with a River View, 2012   161
Safe Hands' Rodent Surprise, 2013   163
A Popular Politician, 2013   165
The Name's Crocodile, Mr Crocodile, 2013   167
Film Crew's Faux Pas, 2013   169
Sonning's First-Class Delivery, 2013   171
Flood Fishing   173

Bibliography   175

INTRODUCTION

'Twenty bridges from Tower to Kew,
Wanted to know what the River knew,
Twenty Bridges or twenty-two,
For they were young, and the Thames was old
And this is the tale that River told.'

The River's Tale by Rudyard Kipling

The 19th-century Member of Parliament John Burns described the Thames as 'liquid history' and ever since the Romans founded Londinium on its banks almost two millennia ago, the river has played a key cultural and economic, political and social role in the history of both England and Europe.

Rising in rural Gloucestershire before emptying into the North Sea on the Essex coast, the 215-mile (346-km) stretch of water is the longest river running solely through England, and over the centuries it has borne witness to some of the country's most spectacular and infamous, unforgettable and bizarre events.

The River Thames' Strangest Tales celebrates the surreal, funny and at times unbelievable events and episodes that have occurred on, beneath and along the banks of the country's most famous waterway.

History, as Burns alluded, seeps through the river. The Thames has been at the heart of countless iconic moments and from the launch of the world's first ever submarine to the sad sight of Admiral Lord Nelson's final journey, the conversion of the Saxons to Christianity to the national mourning that followed the death of Winston Churchill, the river has never been far from the action.

The same could also be said about the careless Roman legionary who dropped his brothel token in the river two thousand years ago.

Politics, too, has frequently enjoyed a close relationship with the river, and the fractious 1937 Parliamentary debate about the exact length of the Thames, the dock workers' strike that inadvertently threatened to flood swathes of Essex and Kent in the 1980s and the unpleasant stink from the water that so discombobulated the noses of the MPs in Parliament in the 19th century all get our vote.

The story of former Deputy Prime Minister John Prescott swimming down the Thames in his wet suit, however, is undoubtedly the political *pièce de résistance* of the book.

Crime and, frequently, punishment have been an integral part of the river's story, and from the prison hulks that once floated on the water, housing the hapless souls destined for deportation, to the creation of the world's first police force to combat endemic thievery, to the unusual case of the *underwater* drug dealers, law and order is to the fore.

As a natural phenomenon, it is only fitting that many of the stories that follow feature the river's indigenous (and sometimes invasive) wildlife. From the 'four great fysshes' that terrorised Londoners in the middle of the 15th century to the hungry, nine-foot shark with an appetite for timepieces, and from the startling discovery of a foreign fish with real bite to the hordes of hairy Chinese crabs clawing away at the banks of the Thames, David Attenborough could not offer a more comprehensive natural history of the river.

Writers, poets and musicians have all been inexorably drawn to the Thames over the years and in the pages that follow it will become evident why *Alice's Adventures in Wonderland* owes a literary debt to the river, how the Sex Pistols found big trouble while on the water in 1977 and why King George I was a manic musical task master.

Sport, too, is synonymous with the river and the stories of what was nearly an abrupt conclusion to the first ever Boat Race in 1829, the record-breaking Doggett's Coat and Badge and the schoolchildren forced to swap their oval balls for oars all make a welcome appearance.

The River Thames' Strangest Tales, however, is a broad church and some of the strangest, truly bizarre stories in its pages defy categorisation or catalogue. They are, in short, laws unto themselves.

The AWOL prop from a James Bond film that had the residents of Reading in palpitations is a case in point. As is the TV vet who took to the river in a giant dog bowl, while the sight of a Lego pharaoh (built from 200,000 of the famous little Danish bricks) floating through London probably had to be seen to be believed.

The postbox which appeared overnight at the bottom of a bridge over the Thames in Berkshire is a mystery that may never be solved, while the explanation why the NASA space shuttle suddenly appeared above the river in Gloucestershire in 1983 is as intriguing as it is surreal.

The tales of the day an elephant walked on the Thames in 1814 or the polar bear who fished for his supper in the river are the proverbial icing on the cake.

The River Thames' Strangest Tales is an affectionate celebration of the rich and often riotous history of the river, the people who have lived beside it and worked on the water, and the events both momentous and seemingly insignificant that have made the Thames such an iconic, world-famous waterway.

THE SAXONS FIND GOD
AD 635

'Those who say religion has nothing to do with politics,' Mahatma Gandhi once observed, 'do not know what religion is.' A perceptive man, Gandhi, and it is true that throughout human history the messy and murky business of politics has been inextricably intertwined with matters of faith.

An early example of this symbiotic if sometimes uneasy relationship was in evidence in the seventh century when Pope Honorius I was cogitating in the Vatican and decided that the process of converting the English to Christianity really needed a bit of a kick-start.

The Pope despatched a Germanic priest by the name of Birinus on a special papal mission to spread the word of God among the heathen West Saxons, and after landing at Southampton in 634, our loyal preacher headed to Dorchester-on-Thames for a meet and greet with King Cynegils, the *grand fromage* of the Saxons.

Cynegils, however, had more pressing political matters on his mind. He desperately wanted to forge an alliance with King Oswald of Northumbria against Penda of Mercia but couldn't quite seal the deal despite a serious charm offensive because Oswald, a Christian, was reluctant to get into bed with a heathen.

Birinus, of course, saw his opportunity and offered to baptise Cynegils, who realised it would be politically expedient for him to find God, and in 635 Birinus waded knee-deep into the Thames near Dorchester and baptised the king and many of his loyal subjects. The West Saxons embraced the Church, Cynegils bestowed Birinus with Dorchester as his episcopal see and the two kingdoms united against the vile menace that was Mercia.

From a religious perspective, it was mission accomplished, but neither Cynegils nor Oswald was to reap the military benefits they envisaged from their *entente cordiale*. Just eight years after his conversion, Cynegils went to meet his new God in person while Oswald was killed and then dismembered after finishing on the losing side of the Battle of Maserfeld against Penda, who comfortably outlived both his Christian enemies.

Which proves that having God on your side in a fight isn't necessarily all it's cracked up to be.

LONDON BRIDGE FALLS DOWN
1091

It was in 1987 that weatherman Michael Fish infamously took to the airwaves to reassure viewers that the country was not about to be battered into submission by a huge storm. 'Earlier on today, apparently, a woman rang the BBC and said she heard there was a hurricane on the way,' he said. 'Well, if you're watching, don't worry, there isn't.' A few short hours later, the Southeast was hit by the worst storm since 1703, leaving 18 dead and Fish's reputation in tatters.

Nearly 900 years earlier contemporary meteorologists fared no better with their predictions when London was devastated by a tornado. In fairness, we can't blame Fish for that one, but it does go to prove it's dangerous to put too much trust in weathermen.

The tornado hit on the morning of 17 October 1091. Modern experts have estimated the winds could have reached speeds in excess of 230mph (370kmph) and the capital's many flimsy wooden structures offered little resistance to the onslaught.

'At the hour of six a dreadful whirlwind from the south east coming from Africa blew upon the City and overthrew upwards of six hundred houses,' recounts The *Chronicles of London Bridge*, published in 1825. 'Several Churches greatly damaged the Tower and tore away the roof and part of the wall of the Church of St Mary-le-Bow in Cheapside. The roof was carried to a considerable distance and fell with such force that several of the rafters being about twenty eight feet [8.5m] in length pierced upwards of twenty feet [6m] into the ground and remained in the same position as when they stood in the Chapel.'

The tornado also had quite a destructive effect on the Thames. 'During the same storm too the water in the Thames rushed along with such rapidity and increased so violently that London Bridge was entirely swept away,' reports the *Chronicles*, 'whilst the lands on each side were overflowed for a considerable distance.'

The sight of the bridge being washed away by the river must have been as spectacular as it was terrifying for Londoners and a poor reflection of the craftsmen who had erected it just 25 years earlier on the orders of William the Conqueror. King William II had it rebuilt but the latest incarnation of London Bridge lasted little longer than its predecessor, burning down in 1136.

It would be another 600 years before the traditional nursery rhyme 'London Bridge Is Falling Down' was first recorded in England but it's not hard to guess where its anonymous creator drew inspiration from.

MATILDA'S FROZEN FLIT
1142

Family relations are a minefield. Simmering sibling rivalries, drunken Christmas rows and tensions about the seating plan for cousin Gertrude's wedding are all potential battlegrounds and it's a rare family indeed that can claim to have escaped entirely such familiar flashpoints. Royal families are not immune to the odd bunfight either, but when the throne is at stake such disputes tend to be particularly bloody and vicious.

A typically bellicose example of feuding nobility occurred back in 1135 when Henry I popped his clogs. The king had publicly named his daughter, Empress Matilda, his heir but her cousin Stephen had other ideas and, on receiving the news of his uncle's death, he decided he quite fancied the top job for himself. Stephen hurriedly decamped from his base in Boulogne, rode to London and, three days before Christmas, cajoled the Archbishop of Canterbury into crowning him the new monarch.

Matilda was absolutely livid and for the next seven years she and her allies launched a series of rebellions in an attempt to depose her cousin. Things came to a head in the winter of 1142 when Matilda was holed up in Oxford Castle, nestled on the banks of the Castle Mill Stream, an offshoot of the Thames. Stephen saw a chance to silence his troublesome relation and Matilda found herself besieged by his troops and apparently without means of escape.

Luck, however, was on her side. Castle Mill was frozen over and in the dead of night, wearing a white dress to camouflage her against the snow, she was lowered out of the castle and onto the ice. Accompanied by four shivering knights, Matilda, ahem, waltzed to the safety of her nearby stronghold at Wallingford.

A cunning ploy indeed, but Stephen ultimately had the last laugh. The intermittent civil war was to last another five years but when her close ally, Robert of Gloucester, died, Matilda decided she had had enough of this particular familial squabble and in 1148 she left England for France, never to return.

The intriguing history of Oxford Castle does not end there, though. After Matilda's icy getaway, the castle became a prison in the 14th century. Much of the original stonework was destroyed during the English Civil War and a new building was constructed on the site in 1785. In the 20th century it became known as HM Prison Oxford before it was finally closed in 1996.

The site is now the home of a new shopping centre and hotel, with the former cells now used as rooms, the first prison in the country to have been converted to accommodate paying guests rather than house members of the criminal fraternity.

AVIAN ARITHMETIC
C. 1150

Whether it is an urban myth or a painful reality that a swan can break a man's arm is debatable. Adrian Mole was convinced of the dangers posed by our large feathered friends in *Weapons of Mass Destruction* and there is anecdotal evidence to suggest it's imprudent to antagonise the big white fellas.

It seems, though, that no one has warned the men and women who take to the Thames each year with the express purpose of locating, corralling and then tagging the river's population of swans in an annual ceremony known as 'Swan Upping'.

Dating back to the 12th century, Swan Upping began as a means by which the reigning monarch could establish how many mute swans were in residence on certain stretches of the Thames. The king or queen had exclusive rights to the birds and, with swans a highly prized dish at feasts in those days, the monarch wanted to know how many oversized roasts he or she could expect on the royal plate. Rowing skiffs were despatched once a year and the number of birds recorded.

The historic practice was tweaked in the 15th century when a Royal Charter gave two London trade associations, the Vintners' Company and Dyers' Company, a share of the fowl bounty and both organisations began despatching their own boats to conduct the feathery census.

The river's swans have been harassed on an annual basis ever since but these days the birds are merely counted, ringed and their health assessed rather than ending up in the oven. Swan Upping is conducted in the third week of July on a 79-mile (127-km) stretch of the Thames that passes through Middlesex, Surrey, Buckinghamshire and Oxfordshire. Six skiffs are deployed for the five-day job, carrying the Royal Swan Uppers, resplendent in their

traditional red uniforms, as well as representatives of the Vintners'
and Dyers' companies. A chorus of 'All up!' is traditionally shouted
when a swan is spotted and the boats race to surround the bird and
slap an identification ring on its leg.

So has a swan, understandably disgruntled at being hauled out of
the river by the Uppers, ever exacted revenge and actually broken an
arm? There are no recorded incidents that have resulted in a trip to
A&E but the birds do attack when the opportunity arises.

The most recent contretemps came in 2005 when Robert Coleman
of the Vintners' Company fell into the water. The swan he had just
caught, tagged and then released spotted his misfortune and
pounced, jumping all over the hapless chap and furiously flapping its
wings. Robert eventually escaped after the swan retreated, apparently
content to have expressed its displeasure.

'This swan decided to get his own back for being tied up,' said an
eye witness to the avian attack. 'It was about ten feet away when it
came chasing back seeming to say, "You are in my territory now."
He came and jumped on him basically.'

A NOT SO DEADLY DUEL
1163

Politics in the 12th century could frequently be a deadly business. There were potentially great rewards for those who managed to successfully climb the greasy pole within the Royal Court but drop the ball (or, in this particular case, the flag) and the consequences could prove terminal.

The Norman nobleman Henry of Essex, learned this lesson the hard way when Henry II took the English throne in 1154 and an unseemly scramble between the country's leading lights began to ingratiate themselves with the new king. Everyone but everyone wanted to be the monarch's new best friend.

Initially Henry's future looked bright when the king made him Sheriff of Buckinghamshire in 1156 but the nobleman made a spectacular faux pas the following year that would ultimately cost him everything.

The king was having a spot of bother with the rebellious Welsh princes Owain Gwynedd and Rhys ap Gruffydd. He despatched an army to show the Welsh who was the daddy and Henry of Essex dutifully tagged along to show his loyalty. Unfortunately, during one battle he dropped the royal standard, which was considered very poor form indeed.

Six years later Henry's butter-fingers came back to haunt him when a political rival by the name of Robert de Montfort accused him of treason, citing his combat clumsiness as evidence of his disloyalty. The king decreed the spat could only be settled through trial by combat and the two men decamped to Fry's Island on the Thames, just south of Reading, for their legalised dust-up.

Sadly Henry proved to be a lover, not a fighter, and when he was struck down by de Montfort's sword, the king ordered the Benedictine monks from nearby Reading Abbey to remove the body.

Why a gaggle of monks were watching a fight to the death is between them and the big man. The monks did what they were told but when they got Henry back to the abbey they discovered he wasn't actually dead and nursed him back to health.

It was now that his luck finally changed. The king declined to insist on a rematch, which hapless Henry would surely have lost, and instead ruled that he must spend the rest of his life at Reading Abbey.

A convicted traitor who was stripped of his money and lands, Henry decided that if you can't beat them, join them, and became a monk himself. He spent the final seven years of his life in the abbey, just a few miles from the banks of the river that had provided the setting for his almost fatal fall from grace.

A POLAR INTERLOPER
1252

London is an unlikely home for a bear. Michael Bond's marmalade-loving Paddington may have found the capital agreeable but he's a fictional children's character; the truth is the Big Smoke isn't really the ideal environment for the muscular members of the *Ursidae* family.

Back in the 13th century, however, it was a rather different story and for a number of years anyone who ventured down to the Thames near the Tower of London could well have been confronted by the unlikely sight of a polar bear fishing for its supper. Yep, a 1500lb (680kg) predator armed with flesh-shredding claws and a mouthful of enormous teeth. In London.

The polar bear (or *Ursus maritimus* if you're fluent in Latin) was a present to Henry III from King Haakon of Norway in 1252. The Tower of London was already home to an expanding menagerie of assorted lions, leopards and hyenas and Haakon presumably thought a polar bear was just what the royal collection needed.

The unusual gift came accompanied by a keeper but once the pomp and ceremony of the presentation were over, there were practicalities to consider. The bear had to be housed and fed and so the king ordered his two Sheriffs of the City of London to take care of everything.

The problem was the polar bear was a hungry bugger, London was not blessed with an abundant supply of seals and it was steadily eating the poor sheriffs out of house and home. The solution was of course obvious. The bear could hunt for its own food in the river and – as long as precautions were taken to ensure it didn't get the opportunity to chow down on the local residents – the plan really didn't have a down side.

'We [the king] command you that for the keeper of our white bear recently arrived from Norway,' wrote Henry, 'ye cause to be had one muzzle and one iron chain to hold the bear without the water, one long strong cord, to hold the same bear fishing or washing himself in the Thames.'

And so a polar bear on a leash, hunting for fish, became a familiar sight in London, proof once again that fact really is stranger than fiction.

THE ROUT AT RADCOT
1387

The Thames has tragically claimed the lives of thousands of innocent people over the years but occasionally it has also provided liquid salvation (see 'Matilda's Frozen Flit') to those in dire straits. The great river can be both killer and saviour and one notable figure who certainly owed his life to the Thames was Robert de Vere, the Duke of Ireland. His story goes something like this.

A close ally of King Richard II, de Vere was accused of treason by a group of ambitious nobles plotting to get him out of the picture and increase their own influence at the Royal Court. Tensions were high and it was only a matter of time before blood was spilled. Robert headed north in 1387 to raise an army and with 15,000 troops at his command he began the march back to London where he would join forces with the king. It was not to be an entirely trouble-free journey.

To reach Richard, de Vere and his soldiers would have to get over the Thames and he opted for Radcot Bridge in Oxfordshire to make his crossing. A rebel army captained by Henry Bolingbroke, the Earl of Derby, was already waiting for him and had destroyed the central arch of the bridge in an attempt to block his passage.

Initially Robert fancied his chances of victory but his timid troops did not share his confidence and when they were surrounded by more of Derby's soldiers coming up from behind, the game was up and they were routed. 'When he came to Radcot Bridge,' wrote the 16th-century chronicler Raphael Holinshed, 'four miles [6.4km] from Chipping Norton, he suddenly espied the army of the lords and finding that some of his troops refused to fight, he began to wax faint hearted, and to prepare to escape by flight, in which he succeeded.'

An estimated 800 of his soldiers were killed, many of them drowning as they desperately tried to flee, but Robert escaped death by plunging into the Thames on his horse. He quickly discarded his armour and sword to lighten the load, forced his mount to swim upstream and, despite the attentions of a unit of Derby's archers, he got away. He spent the night hiding in a nearby wood and eventually slipped away to exile in France.

Robert's second-in-command, Sir Thomas Molineux, was not so lucky. He, too, thought the Thames would save him but as he tried to make his own watery escape, he was spotted by one of Derby's lieutenants, Sir Roger Mortimer, and ordered to get out of the water sharpish.

'If I come, will ye save my life?' Molineux asked, according to Holinshed. 'I will make ye no such promise,' replied Sir Roger, 'but, notwithstanding, either come up or thou shalt presently die for it.' Molineux replied: 'Well then, if there be no other remedy, suffer me to come up, and let me try with hand blows, either with you or some other, and so die like a man.'

His hopes of a heroic death, however, were rather cruelly dashed as he staggered up the river bank only for Sir Roger to pluck off Molineux's helmet and plunge his dagger into his foe's unprotected head.

BEASTS OF THE THAMES
1457

Everyone loves a marine mystery. Do mermaids really exist? When is the Loch Ness Monster going to put in another appearance? Whatever happened to the Bermuda Triangle? And did nearly six million viewers really tune in to watch Dom Joly on 'celebrity' ITV diving show *Splash*?

In 2011 the Thames got in on the act when reports began to roll in of a mysterious predator lurking beneath the water around the Olympic Park in Stratford. An unfortunate Canada goose was spotted being dragged down to the murky depths by an unknown assailant and speculation about the guilty species was rife.

A pet alligator gone rogue was probably the most entertaining theory on offer, while others argued it was a large snake on the loose. More rational people suggested the creature, predictably dubbed the 'killer beast' by the *Daily Mail*, was a peckish pike, a powerful Wels catfish or even a large otter; for a few diverting days, everyone found the story jolly entertaining.

It was not, though, the first time the Thames had found itself the source of a watery teaser. Back in the 15th century Londoners were gripped by terrifying tales of huge aquatic creatures making their home in the river. The year was 1457 and there were several unexplained sightings of four 'great fysshes' which fascinated and frightened the locals in equal measure. No one was sure what the hell they were and it was not until the quartet were caught (we sadly don't know how) days later that the mystery was finally solved.

'They proved to be two whales, a swordfish and a walrus,' wrote the leading British naturalist R. S. R. Fitter in his 1946 book *London's Natural History*. 'If, as seems possible, the "swordfish" was really a narwhal or sea unicorn, all the "great fysshes" were in this case really mammals. All of them were probably eaten, for the meat of whales, porpoises and seals was a regular feature at feasts at this time.'

The unexpected haul would have kept the capital's Ye Olde Fysshe & Chip Shops in business for weeks.

THE BIG CHILL
1608

If we believe the boffins in white coats, global warming is a terrifying prospect that we must collectively avert before the icecaps melt and the seas swell, the world's food-producing fields are reduced to arid desert and David Dickinson's tan gets so deep he becomes indistinguishable from the mahogany sideboards of which he is so fond. Climate change is, we are told, a broad church and we'd all better start praying.

A few hundred years ago, however, our ancestors were faced with contrasting meteorological conditions as Britain was plunged into what is known as the 'Little Ice Age'; between 1500 and the mid-1800s, the UK was jolly chilly indeed. The shareholders of British Gas, EDF, npower *et al.* would have made an absolute killing.

The prolonged cold snap led to bitter winters and in London the remarkable sight of the Thames freezing over. The first record of the river becoming locked solid by ice dates back to AD 250, when it was frozen for nine long weeks, but the Little Ice Age saw the frequency of the amazing freeze increase and in 1536 there are even reports of King Henry VIII travelling down a stationary Thames in his royal sleigh from Westminster to Greenwich. Given his reputation as a 'generously proportioned' monarch, we can only assume the ice that year was reassuringly thick.

In 1608 the river froze once again and it was this year the capital staged its first official 'Frost Fair' on the Thames, a carnival of partying, gaming and gambling, skating, assorted attractions and general merriment on the ice. From 1608 onwards, Londoners would flock to the river whenever it froze and before you could say, 'It's brass monkeys out here,' various stalls, entertainers and acrobats would appear.

One of the severest frosts to hit the capital came in 1684 and the ice on the Thames was measured at 11 inches (28cm) thick. The river was icebound for two full months and, as the renowned diarist John Evelyn recorded, everyone had a whale of a time. 'Coaches plied from Westminster to the Temple,' he wrote, 'and from several other stairs too [sic] and fro, as in the streets; sleds, sliding with skeetes, a bull-baiting, horse and coach races, puppet plays and interludes, cooks, tipling and other lewd places, so that it seemed to be a bacchanalian triumph, or carnival on the water.'

There were, of course, inherent dangers to partying on the ice. In January 1789 melting ice dragged down a ship that was anchored next to a riverside pub, causing the building to collapse and killing five people. In 1814, the last of the official Frost Fairs, some lunatic decided to parade an elephant on the ice although, miraculously, the stunt did not condemn everyone to a watery grave in the process.

A change in the climate in the 19th century and the building up of the river's banks (which caused the Thames to flow significantly faster) saw freezes become an increasing rarity. The river last ground to a wintry halt in the winter of 1962–63 and although there was no actual Frost Fair, Londoners were quick to take advantage of the situation.

The big freeze began on 22 December. Within days the Thames was solid and children, temporarily excused from school, took to the ice to play hockey on their bicycles. Milkmen abandoned their floats in favour of skis to complete their rounds and one bright spark even invented a new sport, towing skiers by car on the frozen river. Happy days, until the thaw finally arrived in March the following year.

There are still Frost Fairs today. The festival was revived in 2003 at Bankside, but the modern version is inevitably a disappointingly land- rather than ice-based event, there's not an elephant in sight and bull-baiting is conspicuous by its absence.

THE UNDERWATER KING
1620

Today it is the oceans and seas that are silently patrolled by the nuclear-powered submarines of the world's most militarised nations but the history of submersible vessels can actually be traced directly back to the dear old River Thames during the reign of King James I.

The first design for a submarine was devised by English mathematician and former Royal Navy gunner William Bourne in his book *Inventions or Devises*, published in 1578. It detailed a rowing boat encased in a wooden frame, covered in waterproof leather, and holes with flexible leather seals to allow the movement of oars. Air came in through long snorkel tubes held above the water's surface by floats.

Sadly, our William popped his clogs before he ever got the chance to turn his idea into a reality, but in 1620 a Dutch boffin by the name of Cornelis Drebbel, who just happened to be working for the Royal Navy at the time, decided he'd pick up Bourne's baton and run with it.

With his first prototype constructed, Drebbel needed somewhere to test it; looking out of the window of his office at Admiralty House, his attention was suddenly caught by a big wet thing called the Thames. The first test run on the river was a huge success. Drebbel's craft was able to stay below the surface for up to three hours, could dive to depths of 16 feet (5m) and was capable of making impressively lengthy journeys.

'He built a ship in which one could row from Westminster to Greenwich,' wrote contemporary Dutch historian Cornelius van der Wonde. 'The distance of two Dutch miles, even five or six miles or as far as one pleased. In this boat a person could see under the surface of the water.'

Over the next four years the Dutchman manufactured two further, more refined prototypes and, according to one writer of the time, he even managed to convince James I to accompany him on one submerged trip, making him the first king in history to travel by submarine. Thousands of Londoners lined the banks of the Thames to witness the royal spectacle, some perhaps expecting to see a bizarre case of watery regicide.

Ironically, the only people who were unimpressed by Drebbel's achievements were the old sea dogs at the Admiralty, who couldn't envisage a military application for his invention, reasoning it would be jolly dangerous to fire a cannon from inside what was essentially a giant leather bag. The Royal Navy let him go and submarine warfare would have to wait until 1776 and the American War of Independence for the first incident of underwater aggression.

A ROSE BY ANY OTHER NAME

c. 1644

Oliver Cromwell is a perennially divisive figure in the story of England's turbulent history. For some he was an unflinching champion of parliamentary freedom and defender of democracy, but many can never forgive or forget his role in the execution of King Charles I, his subsequent orders to melt down the Crown Jewels and his near genocidal treatment of Ireland's Catholics.

He was certainly not a man to be messed with but he did apparently possess a softer side. Cromwell revealed his hitherto secret touchy-feely personality during the English Civil War in the 1640s. All the fighting, running through Royalists and reshaping the political map of the nation was obviously thirsty work and our Oliver decided to recharge his batteries with a swift beer at a picturesque pub by the banks of the Thames in Witney, Oxfordshire.

Legend has it that Cromwell was wearing a rose in a buttonhole of his overcoat but the heat of the day had taken its toll and the flower was wilting, prompting our famous Roundhead to order an extra pint of ale and place his bloom in the glass for a reinvigorating drink. The unconventional floral pick-me-up worked. Cromwell's rose was saved (for a few further hours at least) and as a result drinkers can today enjoy a glass or two down by the Thames in a pub which is now known as the Rose Revived.

It's a good story but to be strictly accurate the inn's Cromwell-inspired moniker did not catch on immediately. The records suggest the pub was called the Fayre Inn, after the biannual fairs held in the area, when Cromwell paid his visit, and it was variously known as the Rose and the Rose and Crown before finally adopting its current, more evocative name sometime in the late 1800s.

The modern pub plays on its history by serving dishes such as Old English Seaside Platter and Beef & Ruddles Ale Pie, but disappointingly the menu is bereft of 'Cromwell's Crispy Chicken' or 'Oliver's Organic Olives'.

THE FAMOUS TROUT
1670s

No one is sure exactly how many pubs and inns hug the banks of the Thames. It would be the mother of all pub crawls to begin at the river's source in Gloucestershire and follow it all the way to the North Sea and it's probably safe to assume anyone who undertook such a task wouldn't be able to remember their own name, let alone how many riverside hostelries there actually are.

One of the most famed pubs by the Thames must be The Trout Inn, just north of Oxford, a Grade II listed building that boasts an intriguing history and may be familiar to you even if you haven't sampled its hospitality in person. Built in the late 17th century, the pub was constructed on the site of a hospice that belonged to Godstow Nunnery, the remains of which still stand on the opposite side of the river, and the frugal builders even purloined some of the stones from the building to finish the Trout.

Since it first opened its doors, the pub has become a firm favourite with Oxford's undergraduates and it was in the 1920s that a young Evelyn Waugh popped in for a pint. The place made such an impression on him that Waugh mentioned the Trout 20 years later in his seminal work *Brideshead Revisited* when the characters Charles Ryder and Sebastian Flyte quench their thirst. The pub is also the scene for a fatal rendezvous in D. L. Murray's 1945 novel *Folly Bridge: A Romantic Tale*.

Other literary patrons of the pub over the years have included C. S. Lewis, author of *The Lion, the Witch and the Wardrobe*, who would 'sit on the wall with the Isis flowing below us and munch cheese and bread'. It is also believed J. R. R. Tolkien, a professor at Oxford as well as the creator of *The Lord of the Rings*, also sank a few on the Trout's riverside terrace.

Acclaimed crime writer Colin Dexter was a regular at the Trout and used it as a backdrop in several of his *Inspector Morse* books. When ITV came to bring Dexter's creation to the small screen the Trout was used for filming, which is why you might just recognise the place even if you've never been there.

The pub's profile received another very public boost in 2001 when former US President Bill Clinton and daughter Chelsea popped in for refreshment. The regulars were no doubt hugely relieved when they realised he'd left his saxophone back in the States.

BADGE OF HONOUR
1715

Raise the topic of competitive rowing on the Thames and for most it will conjure up images of the Boat Race or the Henley Regatta. They are, of course, both fine events steeped in history but both are still mere Johnny-come-latelies in comparison to the river's lesser-known Doggett's Coat and Badge race, the oldest rowing contest on the planet.

First staged back in the early 18th century, the Doggett's Coat and Badge was the brainchild of Thomas Doggett, an Irish actor and comedian who decamped to London in search of fame, fortune and his Equity card. One version of the race's story goes that Thomas fell into the water while crossing the Thames but was rescued by a waterman and subsequently established the event in gratitude for his escape from a watery grave. The second (probably more accurate) version of events is that Doggett founded the race to commemorate the first anniversary of George I's ascension to the English throne.

Whatever the truth, the Doggett's Coat and Badge was born in 1715 and followed a four miles and five furlongs (7,400m) course from London Bridge to Cadogan Pier, Chelsea. The race was open to young watermen in the first year of their professional careers on the Thames and, somewhat masochistically, was run *against* the tide. The prize for the fastest and fittest oarsman was a traditional red waterman's coat boasting a silver badge.

Our Thomas organised and managed the race until he popped his clogs in 1721 but the event did not die with him. He left strict instructions (plus some hard cash) in his will to ensure the Doggett's Coat and Badge could continue, and in 1722 the Fishmonger's Company took charge. They are still organising the annual race today.

There have been changes to the event over the years. Since 1873, the madness that was rowing nearly five miles against the tide was abandoned and the direction of the race reversed, and competitors now use modern single sculls rather than the bigger, more unwieldy passenger boats that were around in Thomas's time. The decrease in the number of modern watermen on the Thames has also seen the qualifying criteria relaxed and rowers are now allowed to enter the race three times rather than the original once-only rule.

The inaugural race of 1715 was won by a chap called John Opey but Thomas was evidently not an avid record-keeper in those early years and the names of several winners are unknown. We do know big Jack Broughton, an English champion bare-knuckle boxer, was the winner in 1730 and that the race finally welcomed the fairer sex in 1992 when Claire Burran became the first woman to compete.

The record winning time was set in 1973 when Bobby Prentice rowed his way to victory in 23 minutes and 22 seconds, which was certainly impressive but a mere sprint compared to the 38 days 11 hours and seven long minutes it took him to row across the Atlantic as part of a 12-man crew in 2010.

A VERY ROYAL
MUSICAL
1717

Some combinations are just meant to be. Gin and tonic. Laurel and Hardy. The sudden onset of a brief British summer and sunburn. Back in 1717, however, it was the world premiere of Handel's famous *Water Music* and its debut performance on a barge sailing serenely up and down the River Thames.

The synchronicity between the title of Handel's composition and the setting was at the behest of the music-loving King George I, who wanted to spend a balmy summer evening being serenaded on the river in London and booked a 50-piece orchestra to perform the Water Music for him for the first time.

And so on 17 July the orchestra cast off on a barge down the Thames closely followed by another boat carrying George and a bevy of beautiful socialites. The musical flotilla, followed by numerous other boats eager to hear Handel's latest work, set off from Whitehall Palace upriver towards Chelsea; on the king's orders, the band struck up.

George liked what he heard. In fact, he liked it so much that the orchestra were instructed to play the entire piece three times before the king finally retired to his bed chamber at gone midnight. According to contemporary chroniclers, the musicians were so worn out by their exertions that many collapsed at the end of what had been a historic but exhausting evening.

Interestingly, our 1717 concert is not the only time the strains of Handel's Water Music have been heard floating down the Thames. In 2010, a group of historians and experts recreated the event when they launched the English Concert orchestra onto the river complete with period costumes and ridiculous wigs.

Two years later, 11 leading British composers collaborated to create New Water Music, an affectionate tribute to Handel based on his original work and performed on the Thames in front of a global audience of millions during the Queen's Diamond Jubilee Pageant.

THE BRIDGE WITH NO EXCISE

1769

The British have an innate and long-standing distaste for paying travel tolls. Our Continental cousins may be happy to part with their hard-earned euros for the privilege of driving down the motorway but here in Blighty we tend to frown on being asked to pay extra on our journey.

The Severn Bridge, the Dartford Crossing and the M6 Toll may be money-grabbing exceptions to our frugal habits but, on the whole, Brits keep their wallets firmly tucked away en route to visiting Aunt Edna or B&Q.

Pity then the motorists who regularly have to use the B4044 in Oxfordshire. It's a scenic enough route but when the road approaches the Thames they must use Swinford Bridge to avoid flooding their engines. For the privilege, they must part with the princely sum of five pence each and every time.

The story of how the bridge became a fail-safe money-spinner goes something like this.

In 1767, King George III was in the neighbourhood. The monarch wanted to cross the river but there was no bridge and the ford at Swinford was looking decidedly iffy after heavy rain and flooding. Contemporary accounts of exactly what happened next differ, with some reporting that George fell into the river and others chronicling how his carriage got stuck in the mud; the upshot was the king was not amused.

He summoned the local big cheese, the Earl of Abingdon, and demanded he build a bridge for the convenience of all those wishing to cross the Thames at Swinford. George of course meant for his own royal convenience but the Earl protested, claiming poverty and a lack of cement. George, however, knew how to sweeten a proposition and promised Abingdon he could keep all the tolls he accrued from traffic over the bridge. To seal the deal, he also issued a royal decree enshrining his assertion that the income would be tax-free and that no rival crossing could be constructed within three miles (4.8km) of Swinford. The earl suddenly found the money required for the work and in 1769 Swinford Bridge was opened, charging tuppence a time to cross.

The bridge continues to bring home the bacon today despite tolls for pedestrians being abolished in 1835.

In 2009, it was put up for sale and at a glitzy auction at the Park Lane Hotel in London, an anonymous bidder stumped up £1.08 million to buy the bridge. It might sound a hefty asking price but with an estimated four million cars using the crossing each year, generating a tax-free revenue in the region of £190,000 per annum, it wouldn't take long for the publicity-shy new owner to turn a profit.

FELONS AFLOAT
1776

The debate about the UK's penal system and overcrowding in prisons has long been a bit of a political hot potato. The problem is it costs money to build jails and, as every politician is all too aware, it's damn tricky to convince suspicious voters to part with their hard-earned cash to provide criminals with board and lodging.

In 2004, the Metropolitan Police Service (they don't call it 'Force' any more in case punters get scared) suggested locking up the capital's offenders on a floating prison ship moored on the Thames. It would, they argued, be a cost-effective way of ensuring the safety of law-abiding tax payers – and if the lags behaved themselves, they might even get a cruise down to Southend for good behaviour.

The plan never materialised but the idea of floating prison ships in London was far from a new one. In the late 18th century, the river was awash with criminals incarcerated on ships on the Thames – known as 'hulks' – and it was all a direct result of the American War of Independence.

The policy of housing prisoners on the water began in 1776 when the Yanks declared independence. The move meant the government could no longer ship the country's miscreants over the Atlantic to teach them a lesson and suddenly prisons were bursting at the seams with offenders with nowhere to go.

It was estimated that an extra thousand prison places each year would be needed now that the States was off limits, so, rather than build new jails, the government opted for the cheaper option and the hulks were brought into service. A temporary Act of Parliament (which actually lasted 80 years) was hurriedly passed to make it all legal and respectful and keep the human rights lobby quiet, and the first convicts were despatched to the Thames.

At the same time, the government decided Australia would become Blighty's new dumping ground for criminals and the vast majority of those who found themselves on the hulks were merely waiting for the next transport ship heading down under. In 1798, 1,400 of the 1,900 scheduled for deportation were held on the river.

Life on board was tough. Between 1776 and 1795, an estimated 2,000 of the 6,000 prisoners on the hulks died before stepping on dry land again, a mortality rate of a third, and those who did survive were put to work dredging the river and building docks.

James Hardy Vaux was a prisoner on a hulk prophetically called *Retribution* in the early 1800s and chronicled the appalling conditions awaiting 'guests' on the ship. 'There were confined in this floating dungeon nearly 600 men, most of them double-ironed,' he wrote:

> The reader may conceive the horrible effects arising from the continual rattling of chains, the filth and vermin naturally produced by such a crowd of miserable inhabitants.

> On arriving on board, we were all immediately stripped and washed in two large tubs of water, then, after putting on each a suit of coarse slop clothing, we were ironed and sent below; our own clothes being taken from us.

> Every morning all the convicts capable of work, or in fact, all who are capable of getting into the boats, are taken ashore to the Warren, in which the Royal Arsenal and other public buildings are situated, and there employed at various kinds of labour.

> The guards are commonly of the lowest class of human beings; wretches devoid of feeling; ignorant in the extreme, brutal by nature and rendered tyrannical and cruel by the consciousness of the power they possess. They invariably carry a large and ponderous stick, with which, without the smallest provocation they fell an unfortunate convict to the ground and frequently repeat their blows long after the poor fellow is insensible.

Escape attempts were common but their success varied. In 1776 five men made it off the *Justitia* but two were killed, one injured and the other two recaptured; and while many of the 22 who made it to shore in 1777 got as far as Epping Forest, the majority were eventually rounded up and hanged. Which probably qualifies as a fail.

The barbaric conditions slowly swayed public opinion against the policy and when the *Defense*, the last working hulk, was burned to a cinder at Woolwich Docks in 1857, the era of floating prisons was over and London's wrongdoers finally returned to terra firma.

THE PUNCTUAL SHARK
1787

Anyone who has watched Steven Spielberg's 1975 blockbuster *Jaws* will remember the scene in which Richard Dreyfuss' character dissects a dead shark, opens up its stomach and pulls out a car number plate followed by a tin can. 'He didn't eat a car, did he?' Chief Brody nervously asks. 'Naw, a shark's like a garbage can, it'll eat anything,' replies Hooper. 'Someone probably threw that in a river.'

The omnivorous tendencies of the shark family were also very much in evidence in late 18th-century London when stunned fishermen near Poplar hooked themselves a killer fish and made a startling discovery.

Sharks were, of course, incredibly rare in the Thames, though apparently not completely unprecedented, but the truly 'strange' element of this story is the silver watch they found in the shark's belly. Stranger still was the fact the watch bore the inscription 'Henry Warson, London' and the number '1369'.

The news of the shark and its ill-advised attempt to devour the silver timepiece inevitably found its way into the newspapers and not long later our Henry Warson, a jeweller, came forward and confirmed he had made the watch and sold it to a Mr Ephraim Thompson of Whitechapel, who had given it to his son as a present ahead of his maiden journey to sea on a merchant ship. Thompson Junior sadly never made it home.

'About three leagues off Falmouth, through a sudden heel of the vessel during a squall, young Thompson fell overboard and was no more seen,' relates *London Online*. 'The news of his being drowned reached his family, who little thought that they would ever hear of him again.

'Mr Thompson, senior, bought the shark, not for the sake of having it buried in consecrated ground, but to preserve it as a memorial of so singular an event. It was the largest shark ever remembered to have been taken in the Thames, being from the tip of the snout to the extremity of the tail 9 feet 3 inches [2.8m].'

We are none the wiser about the species of shark that presumably helped himself to the hapless young sailor. There is also no record of the significance of the number 1369, but the story does prove that – like the (fame) hungry contestants on *I'm A Celebrity ... Get Me Out Of Here!* – sharks really will eat absolutely anything.

THAMES FLOWS
THE WRONG WAY
1792

One of what we consider the immutable, unquestionable facts about the Thames is that it flows from west to east. The direction of the river is one of the characteristics that defines it and, although the tidal sections of the Thames below Teddington Lock, 55 miles (89km) away from the coast, ensure it does ebb and flow on a daily basis, the water is inexorably heading towards the North Sea sooner or later.

Except, that is, in the late 18th century when a significant volume of the unsuspecting river suddenly found itself heading in completely the opposite direction, destined – however unlikely it might sound – for an improbable rendezvous with the River Severn and, by definition, the Bristol Channel. It's crazy but it's true.

The key to the mystery is the Thames and Severn Canal, a name that already suggests a possible answer. Built in 1789, the canal was part of a grander scheme to link London with Bristol by man-made waterways; as a result, the most easterly point of the canal began near Thames Head in Gloucestershire, the traditional starting point of the Thames (see 'Going the Extra Fourteen Miles').

It was a frightfully clever scheme but there was a major problem. The initial stages of the Thames and Severn Canal were dug out of porous limestone and the canal was leaking at an alarming rate, an estimated 1.1 million gallons (5 million litres) per day. The engineers had planned to replenish the canal from the River Frome, the River Churn and the River Coln, complemented by assorted springs, but the canal proved leakier than a Cabinet committee meeting and the water continued to disappear.

The hurried solution was to build a pumping station at Thames Head and in 1792 a massive Boulton & Watt steam engine was installed to begin the task of sending the Thames Head's liquid resources into the canal.

And so, dear reader, water destined to make a graceful 215-mile (346-km) journey from Gloucestershire to Essex, taking in the sights of London along the way, suddenly found itself heading west along the Thames and Severn Canal and, via the Stroudwater Navigation, to the Severn Estuary and God knows where after that.

The Thames and Severn Canal, however, never attracted the traffic its backers had hoped for and closed as a commercial operation in 1933. The pumping station at Thames Head is long gone and the Thames is once again at liberty to flow in the direction nature intended.

THE RIVER BEAT
1798

We have already explored how the Thames played a major role in the London prison system during the 18th century (see 'Felons Afloat') but the river boasts another, even more significant claim to fame when it comes to upholding law and order. The Thames gave birth to the oldest police force in the world.

The year was 1798 and the Port of London was the busiest and most lucrative on the planet, the hub of the frenetic trading and global transportation system that built the British Empire. The docks were awash with ships from the West Indies, the Americas, the Far East and India, and every single one of them was groaning under the weight of its exotic cargo of spices, rum, coffee, sugar, silks and tobacco. Coal barges from Newcastle and ships laden with fish from the North Sea merely added to the phenomenal activity that engulfed Wapping.

The Port was an economic nirvana for the merchants who eagerly plied their trade at the docks, but it was also a thieves' paradise and by the end of the 18th century things were getting out of hand. The West India Planters company alone was estimated to be losing an astronomical £250,000 a year as the result of light-fingered workers, and 11,500 of the Port's 33,000 dockers, known then as lumpers, were believed to be thieves.

It was even worse downstream from the Port where ships going in both directions were frequently waylaid by pirates at knifepoint, the robbers having been tipped off in advance by the lumpers about the richest pickings.

Law and order on the Thames was in desperately short supply but that all changed in 1798 when John Harriot, a Justice of the Peace in Essex, joined forces with a London magistrate by the name of Patrick Colquhoun and approached the West India Planters, as well as the West India Merchants company, with a proposal to establish a dedicated police force for the river. The two companies agreed to fund the force for a year and, after attaining government approval, the Thames River Police was formed in June that year.

It was spectacularly successful. The force's patrols on the river in rowing galleys combined with officers at the docks themselves cut crime levels dramatically. In fact, it was so effective that a riot broke out in October outside their HQ in Wapping, stirred up by disgruntled lumpers who suddenly found their 'extra income' had disappeared, and one river policeman was shot dead in the melee. Harriot ordered his officers to fire shots in the air to disperse the angry crowd; in the aftermath, one of the ringleaders was hanged and six others deported down under. The Thames River Police had established its authority and never looked back.

The unit is still in existence today (now called the Metropolitan Police Marine Policing Unit) and predates the formation of the Metropolitan Police by 31 years, thereby making it the world's oldest Old Bill.

GRAND DESIGNS
1802

It's a long time since the heyday of the British Empire. To steal a theme from the *Star Wars* scene where Darth Vader cuts down Obi Wan Kenobi, America (the former student) has now become the master, while those oil-rich chaps from the Middle East and 1.3 billion Chinese now boast the kind of financial and architectural might that were once the preserve of dear old Blighty. The world's richest countries today are building ever bigger, more lavish and more expensive edifices to reflect their new status and whether it's another behemoth of a hotel in Dubai, a skyscraper in Moscow or an entire new city in China, the new order are not afraid to publicly splash their cash.

But back in the 19th century it was the British who were the experts in architectural one-upmanship and for 150 years there was no greater reflection of the nation's confidence, success and wealth than the West India Docks, the final port of call for the countless ships that ploughed their way up the Thames every year.

The scale and cost of the docks was mind-blowing. Officially opened in August 1802, the enormous complex of buildings and moorings adjacent to the river stretched for almost a mile and the whole construction cost £1.2 million (£82 million in today's money), making the West India Docks the most expensive building project in the world at the time. The number of bricks alone needed to raise all the warehouses from their foundations ran into the tens of millions.

The impetus behind the unprecedented project came from a man called Robert Milligan, a ship owner and fabulously rich West Indies merchant. The number of vessels discharging their precious cargo at London's chaotic and overcrowded riverside docks had trebled during the 18th century and Milligan was increasingly eager to get his boats in and out of London in a far more shipshape and profitable way.

He was also fed up with the volume of his cargo that was being pilfered (see 'The River Beat') while his boats were detained at the old docks, so after lobbying a group of like-minded merchants, plantation owners and slave traders with a similar eye for the bottom line, he approached Parliament for permission to begin the big build on the Isle of Dogs. The MPs gave the green light and within two years the West India Docks were a reality.

Milligan and his cohorts now grew even richer as their cargo ships were able to disgorge their valuable loads far faster and get back to sea without undue delay, but life for the casual dock workers who humped the cargoes of sugar, rum and coffee was back-breaking and poorly paid. Moving the imported sugar was a particularly unwelcome gig as the abrasive powder tended to leak from the sacks and rub against the shoulders and hands, earning the quayside the nickname 'Blood Alley'. The dockers definitely didn't get free health care or two weeks' holiday in August either.

The expansion of the Tilbury Docks downstream in Essex in the 20th century and the increasing use of containers (which were too big for West India) saw the docks' fortunes fade. In 1980 the final ship sailed off and the last man out was politely asked to turn out the lights. The area today is reborn as Canary Wharf, the workplace for an estimated 93,000 people and a bustling, vibrant 97-acre site (except that is on weekends when all the bankers are relaxing in the Cotswolds).

NELSON'S FINAL JOURNEY
1806

Whether Lord Nelson did indeed utter the immortal words 'Kiss me, Hardy' on his deathbed in 1805 is a moot point. A man who's just been shot by a French rifleman and is moments from meeting his Maker can be forgiven for rambling. According to contemporary accounts, Captain Hardy was happy to oblige, so everyone was apparently happy.

Moments later Nelson shuffled off this mortal coil. Not of course before masterminding the Royal Navy's crushing defeat of the much larger French and Spanish fleets at the Battle of Trafalgar, but he paid the ultimate price for his triumph and his flagship HMS Victory was charged with the sad task of conveying his body back to Britain. The story goes that Nelson's body was embalmed in brandy, but his thirsty sailors were so desperate for a drink, they frequently had a surreptitious sip on the long journey home.

A state funeral was hurriedly planned and, as befitted a hero who had forged his reputation on the water, it was decided the procession from the Royal Hospital for Seamen at Greenwich, where Nelson was laid in state, to the Admiralty in Whitehall should take place on the Thames. It's what he would have wanted.

The procession embarked on 8 January 1806. Nelson's body travelled on a black-canopied funeral barge accompanied by an impressive flotilla of more than 60 boats, including the Lord Mayor's barge.

The intriguing element of the story, however, is the coffin Nelson was carried in. Or, more accurately, the four coffins that were made for the big, albeit sombre, occasion, the funereal equivalent of Russian dolls. The 'inner' coffin was made from wood salvaged from the mast of the French flagship *L'Orient*, a boat that was blown out of the water by Nelson at the Battle of the Nile in 1798. A second, larger, coffin was a simple lead affair and this, in turn, was lowered into another wooden casket. The first three were then housed in a large gilt coffin, the one that the thousands of mourners would actually see.

Nelson and his four coffins spent the night at the Admiralty after his final trip down the Thames and the following day he was escorted to St Paul's Cathedral by a guard of 10,000 assembled soldiers and interred.

A re-enactment of Nelson's waterbourne procession was staged in 2005 to mark the 200th anniversary of the Battle of Trafalgar and once again the river was thronged with a flotilla of vessels following behind a funeral barge, although this time there was not even one coffin on board.

'Lord Nelson's funeral was an extraordinary occasion such as London had never before witnessed,' said organiser Peter Warwick. 'To begin to convey an idea of how awesome the spectacle was, one has to roll the funerals of Queen Victoria and Diana, Princess of Wales, into one. Queen Victoria's encapsulates the scale of the affair and Diana's captures the immense outpouring of national grief that followed the news of the beloved Nelson's death.'

BOAT RACE STARTS WITH A BANG
1829

The Boat Race is something of a Marmite sporting event. Its supporters claim the annual jaunt down the Thames is the pinnacle of rowing and the envy of the world, while its detractors dismiss it as nothing more than an anachronistic celebration of privilege as 16 muscular toffs huff and puff their way to the finishing line, cheered on by hordes of overexcited chinless wonders.

The famous race can trace its history back to 1829 when Charles Merivale, a student at St John's College, Cambridge, got in touch with his chum Charles Wordsworth of Christ Church, Oxford, who also happened to be the nephew of Lakes poet William (not that his famous relation has any relevance to this particular story).

The two Charlies were old pals from their days at school together at Harrow and decided it would be a jolly wheeze for Cambridge and Oxford to have a rowing contest on the Thames from Hambledon Lock to Henley Bridge, a modest distance of 2¼ miles (3.6km).

The stage – and date, 10 June – was set for the first ever Boat Race. It did not enjoy the most auspicious of starts as both crews allowed the adrenalin and sense of competition to get the better of them and the two boats suffered an embarrassing crash in the embryonic stages of the race.

'We lost the toss and consequently the bank side,' wrote Wordsworth. 'But we made a splendid start and by the time we reached the [Temple] island, having gained a boat's length, our coxswain (a very good one on the Oxford river) being impatient to strike in and place us on the landward side, a foul took place and we had to start afresh.'

Luckily there was no serious damage to either boat or the rowers and, after a cooling-off period, the race was restarted. Oxford were once again the quicker of the two out of the blocks but this time there was no unseemly collision and Wordsworth's crew romped to a convincing victory, finishing in a time of 14 minutes 40 seconds.

There was a seven-year wait before the race was staged for a second time but Cambridge had clearly been practising during the hiatus and avenged their 1829 defeat with victory by 20 lengths in 1836. The race has been a yearly event (World Wars permitting) since 1856, much to the delight of the pub landlords along the banks of the Thames, whose sales of Pimms go through the roof in late March or early April.

THE KILLER RIVER
1858

London would be nothing without the Thames. The river has been the lifeblood of the city ever since the Romans founded Londinium in AD 43, a liquid superhighway that over the years has suckled the city and seen it grow into a major world player. In 1858, however, the Thames dramatically turned on the capital with fatal results.

Not to put too fine a point on it, the crisis was precipitated by too many Number Twos. Human waste. Excrement. Faeces. London was drowning in effluent.

For centuries the Thames had uncomplainingly carried away the residents' unwanted emissions but the early 19th century saw the capital's population soar to 2.5 million and that, of course, meant a lot more bottoms. The great river was already straining under its unpleasant workload and the growing popularity of the flushing toilet merely exacerbated the problem, adding yet more material to the filthy water.

A deadly cholera outbreak that began in Soho in 1854 was a warning sign that all was not well. Things reached a head in 1858. It was a particularly hot, humid summer and as the temperature rose, the sewage that had accumulated in the Thames began to ferment and fester, creating an unholy smell that hung over the city and became known as 'the Great Stink'.

The offensive odour was bad enough but worse was to follow when reports of a cholera outbreak began to surface, the first victim going down in Soho. 'His heart stopped beating barely twenty-four hours after showing the first symptoms of cholera,' wrote Steven Johnson in his book *The Ghost Map: The Story of London's Most Terrifying Epidemic*. 'Within a few hours, another dozen Soho residents were dead.'

Panic quickly began to spread and even MPs at the House of Commons could not escape the pervasive smell that had London in its grip. 'The intense heat had driven our legislators from those portions of their buildings which overlook the river,' reported *The Times* on 18 June that summer. 'A few members, bent upon investigating the matter to its very depth, ventured into the library but they were instantaneously driven to retreat, each man with a handkerchief to his nose.'

It was one thing for London's sewage to be killing the plebs, but causing a pong in Parliament was the final straw. Something had to be done sharpish and Parliament hurriedly passed a bill to overhaul the city's woefully inadequate and ad hoc sewage system and replace it, at great expense, with an infrastructure fit for purpose.

Step forward the man with the plan, Joseph Bazalgette, the chief engineer of the Metropolitan Commission of Sewers. Bazalgette realised that the new, long-overdue system had to get the effluent far away from the city and he designed a hugely ambitious building project consisting of 82 miles (132km) of underground brick main sewers and 1,100 miles (1,770km) of street sewers to get the job done. The human waste would still eventually be dumped untreated in the Thames, but it would be downstream from the city where it was not a threat to public health. Although not fully completed, Bazalgette's new sewer system was officially opened by Edward, Prince of Wales, in 1865.

Thousands of Londoners sadly died from cholera during the 'Great Stink' but Bazalgette's vision eventually proved to be a life-saver as a grateful Thames began to slowly cleanse itself and the dreaded smell receded. It would be many years before the river fully recovered but the journey to its position today as one of the world's cleanest rivers flowing through a major city was well under way.

THE TWO ALICES
1862

There are countless examples of literary classics that nearly never made it into print. H. G. Wells' manuscript for *The War of the Worlds* was initially rejected by publishers as too nightmarish, J. K. Rowling's *Harry Potter and the Philosopher's Stone* was repeatedly dismissed as too long for a children's book and Vladimir Nabokov all but gave up on getting *Lolita* published because of its taboo subject matter. And had it not been for a boat trip down the Thames, the iconic *Alice's Adventures in Wonderland* would never have seen the light of day.

First published in 1865 and written by the Reverend Charles Dodgson under his pen name Lewis Carroll, *Alice* has now sold millions of copies worldwide, but the journey from the germ of the idea for Alice's fantastical subterranean adventures to actual publication all began three years earlier on a rowing boat on the river.

Dodgson was a long-standing friend of a family by the name of Liddell and on a summer's day in 1862, the reverend took to the Thames near Oxford with a 10-year-old Alice Liddell and her sisters for a picnic. Alice asked Dodgson to entertain the girls with a story as they floated along and he duly regaled them with his magical tale of a young girl who fell into a rabbit hole and encountered all manner of strange characters.

It was not the first time the girls had heard this particular story but this time Alice asked the clergyman to commit it to paper. Dodgson was clearly not the most speedy of authors but by November 1864 he had finally finished the job and presented Alice with a manuscript entitled *Alice's Adventures Under Ground*.

Emboldened by Alice's fascination with the story, the Rev also sent the manuscript to a friend, the author George MacDonald, whose own brood were equally enamoured by the antics of the Cheshire Cat, the Knave of Hearts and the Mock Turtle, and a publisher was found for what was to become one of the most popular children's books of all time.

The Thames connection with *Alice in Wonderland*, however, does not end there. Dodgson was well acquainted with the small Oxfordshire village of Binsey, nestled on the banks of the river, and turned to the place for literary inspiration. The village's healing well thus became the 'treacle well' in the book, while Alice Liddell's governess Miss Prickett, a resident of Binsey, provided the template for the Red Queen.

THE FEAR OF
FLOODS
1868

The sheer power and scale of the Thames means the threat of flooding is a fact of life for all those who make their home near the river. Many rural areas witness water cascading over the river's banks each year and even London's imposing defences have been breached in the past (see 'Water, Water, Everywhere').

The Thames will never be truly tamed but it has been subdued. The opening of the Thames Barrier in 1982 was a major victory for man over nature and today the Environment Agency boasts a cornucopia of state-of-the art monitoring devices, interactive maps and other frightfully clever gizmos to predict potential flood hotspots. The river rarely enjoys the element of surprise these days.

Back in the 19th century, however, the business of predicting flooding in the capital was at best basic, and if you take a stroll down to the Victoria Embankment, between the Houses of Parliament and Blackfriars Bridge, you can still see remnants of the Victorian era's disarmingly simple early-warning system.

Peer over the side of the raised wall north or south of the river and you will see a series of cast-iron lion heads, mounted in the stone, each with a mooring ring in its mouth. They are fixed on lamppost pedestals close to the level of the pavement and legend has it that should the lions become submerged by the Thames, the city will inevitably flood. Known as the 'Thames Lions', they were designed by the sculptor Timothy Butler and installed as part of Joseph Bazalgette's great overhaul of London's arcane sewerage system (see 'The Killer River').

It really couldn't have been more straightforward but there is a rhyme connected to the lions, presumably to jog the memory of anyone who may have forgotten exactly how it all worked. 'When the lions drink, London will sink,' it goes. 'When it's up to their manes, we'll go down the drains.'

There is a third line to the rhyme. 'When the water is sucked,' it continues, 'you can be sure we're all . . . in trouble,' but it is unclear whether it is genuinely original or a more modern addition by someone with an uncouth sense of humour.

GOING UNDERGROUND
1876

There are many words in the otherwise beautiful English language that suffer from overuse. 'Literally', 'awesome' and 'mental' are serial offenders, 'ironic' has become all but meaningless, while 'antidisestablishmentarianism' has been hijacked by quiz geeks.

'Iconic' is another word that has lost much of its resonance from excessive use, but we can surely all agree that when applied to Tower Bridge, it's doing the job that God intended. If Tower Bridge ain't iconic, nothing is.

A stately combination of a bascule bridge (opening upwards at the middle) and a suspension bridge, it is elegantly clad in Cornish granite and Portland stone and it's been part of the London landscape since it was officially opened in June 1894. Tower Bridge is now as synonymous with the capital as Beefeaters, Buckingham Palace and exorbitant parking charges.

It's not exactly a 'strange' tale though is it? True, but things get more interesting when you learn that Tower Bridge could conceivably have been 'Tower Tunnel' had the suits at the City of London Corporation decided to go in a radically different direction back in 1876.

London was in desperate need of a new crossing over (or perhaps under) the Thames in the late 19th century. The city's success had brought rapid expansion, traffic was clogging the streets and the pressure on the river's existing bridges was near breaking point. Something had to be done and the City Corporation invited proposals for designs for a new crossing.

A member of the Institute of Civil Engineers by the name of John Standfield came forward. Admittedly his concept for a low-lying tunnel, complete with two enormous Gothic towers at either end and a hydraulic platform to lower and lift travellers up to and down from the surface, was not exactly what the Corporation had anticipated but it certainly won full marks for ingenuity.

Unfortunately, however, for Standfield, his designs were just one of 50 pitches to the Corporation and, after due deliberation, the board members decided to go with something a bit more 'bridgey'. Work began on Tower Bridge in 1886 and after £1.18 million was spent, 70,000 tonnes of concrete poured and 11 tonnes of steel riveted in place, it took a mere eight years to get the job finished.

An oil painting of Standfield's vision for his Thames Tunnel still exists and in 2012 it was put up for auction by Christie's. Experts valued the work at £4,000 but it eventually fetched £10,625, which probably provided scant consolation to Standfield as he watched proceedings from his great drawing board in the sky.

TOO CLOSE TO CALL

1877

The inaugural Boat Race may not have gone exactly according to plan (see 'Boat Race Starts with a Bang') but that unscheduled collision back in 1829 did nothing to damage the race's burgeoning popularity and today, aside from that idiotic Australian protester in 2012, it is a carefully choreographed and seamless event from start to lung-bursting finish.

Back in its formative years, however, the race adopted a distinctly more laissez-faire approach to rules, regulations and, indeed, who the hell had actually won.

It is 1877 and the race is in full swing. Oxford are in front but they hit rough water just after Barnes Bridge and one of their blades is damaged. Cambridge sense blood and up their stroke rate to 40 per minute, inexorably eating into the lead; as both crews power to and then over the finishing line, it's neck and neck. The two boats begin to celebrate, both claiming victory, and all eyes turn to 'Honest' John Phelps, the professional waterman who was responsible for adjudging the winner, for the all-important verdict.

According to some reports, Phelps was asleep under a bush by the banks of the Thames at the crucial moment. Other accounts have him in a skiff which had floated downstream, obscuring his view. What we do know is there were no posts or flags to denote the actual finishing line and, whether he was in the land of Nod or just out of position, hapless John had dropped a bit of a clanger.

With the two crews and the crowd pressing around him, he eventually declared a 'dead heat to Oxford by five feet', which surely qualifies as one of the most unsatisfactory results in the history of sport.

Representatives of Oxford and Cambridge subsequently met the race umpire, Mr Chitty QC, at the Law Courts to sort out the whole sorry mess, but Chitty was not about to rock the boat and ruled the dead heat would stand. Unsurprisingly, 1877 was the last year that John Phelps was invited to act as judge and the debacle also saw the introduction of posts at Mortlake to clearly denote the finishing line.

The Boat Race was staged for the 159th time in 2013 and, thanks to the judgement of 'Honest' John, the head-to-head record now reads 81 successes to Cambridge, 77 wins for Oxford and one baffling and bizarre draw.

THE AGONY OF THE *ALBION*
1898

The 1890s were a tense time in Anglo-German relations. The two big European powers weren't exactly seeing eye-to-eye and while it was not until 1914 that political hostility would become open conflict, both nations could sense trouble brewing.

One result was a frenetic naval arms race. Sea power would be crucial if or when the two countries traded blows and while warships on either side would claim thousands of lives during the First World War, the HMS *Albion* tragically killed 38 much earlier and much closer to home.

The *Albion* was commissioned by the Royal Navy from the Thames Ironworks and Shipbuilding Company. Its yard was located in East London where the Thames met Bow Creek and after months of frantic work the warship was finally ready to be launched. The date was 21 June 1898 and an estimated 30,000 patriotic spectators descended on the yard to witness the launch of the latest addition to the fleet. The Duchess of York was the guest of honour and local workers and schoolchildren had been given the day off to attend.

After three failed attempts to smash the obligatory bottle of champagne on the ship's hull, the Duchess finally did the honours, the yard workers cut the ropes and the Albion, all 600 tonnes of her, rolled downwards. The impact of the vessel on the water created a huge wave, which swept towards the narrow Bow Creek. It was here that around 200 people, eager to get a good view of proceedings, had gathered on a temporary wooden walkway; when the wave hit, it collapsed and threw the poor souls into the water.

Tragically, the rescue effort was hampered because the noise of the crowd celebrating the launch largely drowned out the screams and cries for help, and the all-important launch of the rescue boats was delayed.

In total, 38 Londoners drowned that day, including women and children. Other sources put the death toll at 34 but the revised figure does little to diminish the tragedy. Today a huge ship's anchor in East London Cemetery stands as a tribute to all those people who lost their lives.

CELEBRITY ISLAND

1912

There have been few films in the history of British cinema as controversial or as vilified as Stanley Kubrick's 1971 classic *A Clockwork Orange*. Its infamous, graphic portrayal of violence and rape saw Warner Brothers withdraw the film from British screens for 27 years and the *Daily Mail* almost imploded when they watched a preview copy.

One of the most iconic scenes in the movie sees Alex and his Droogs indulging in a spot of 'ultra violence' with Billyboy and his gang. It's admittedly a tough watch but relevant to our Thames theme as it was filmed on Tagg's Island, a fascinating patch of dry land that lies right in the middle of the river just upstream from Hampton Court Palace.

The story of how the island became a film set began in 1912 when the famed theatre impresario Fred Karno, the man credited with discovering Charlie Chaplin and Stan Laurel and who, legend has it, invented the custard-pie-in-the-face gag, decided he would build a luxurious hotel and entertainment complex right in the middle of the Thames. After buying the island, he bulldozed the existing hotel and commissioned the renowned architect Frank Matcham to design him a new one.

Karno rather immodestly dubbed his new place 'The Karsino' and in May 1913 it opened for business. Sadly, Karno proved a poor businessman and was declared bankrupt in 1925, and for the next 40 or so years the hotel changed hands as well as names, variously going under the moniker of the Palm Beach, the Thames Riviera Hotel and the Casino Hotel.

By the 1970s it was derelict and Kubrick decided the shabby, faded grandeur of the hotel's old ballroom was the perfect backdrop for *A Clockwork Orange*'s big fight scene. It was to prove the building's last hurrah and a year after the cameras had rolled, Karno's grand folly was demolished. The island is now home to 62 houseboats and a community of 100 residents.

Tagg's Island's celebrity connection, however, does not stop there. When Karno first visited the island, he decided he simply had to have his own houseboat and in 1911 he spent £20,000, a huge amount back then, on an opulent vessel complete with panelled cabins and marble bathrooms.

The *Astoria*, as she was christened, had to of course go when Fred went bankrupt, and after a few careful owners, she was bought by Pink Floyd guitarist Dave Gilmour in 1986 and turned into a recording studio. The band partly recorded their albums *A Momentary Lapse of Reason* and *The Division Bell* while floating on the Thames.

The *Astoria* is still moored on the river near Hampton, a longer-lasting legacy to Karno than his ill-fated attempt to make it big in the hotel world.

THE SUB THAT DIDN'T SINK
1918

The Thames is no stranger to submarines. The prototype for the world's first sub was publicly put through its aquatic paces in the river in the early 17th century (see 'The Underwater King') and nearly 300 years later the Thames witnessed the arrival of another underwater craft, which also created a considerable stir in London.

The submarine in question was a German U-boat captured during the First World War, and the story of how it came to be put on show at Temple Pier in the heart of the capital is one containing a splash of comedy, a sprinkling of heroism and a healthy dollop of propaganda.

Launched in the summer of 1915, the U-boat (the *UC-5*) was a minelayer credited with sinking 29 Allied ships totalling 36,288 tons. It was also believed to be the first U-boat to penetrate the English Channel, laying 12 mines off the French coast, and was generally proving to be a thorough irritation in the *derrière*.

Its luck ran out, however, in 1916 when the *UC-5* became stranded on a sandbank off the Suffolk coast, and things went from bad to worse when a passing destroyer, the HMS *Firedrake*, came across the unusual sight of a German sub brazenly on the surface in daylight.

'It was noticed that the whole of the crew of the submarine appeared to be on deck,' reported *The Naval and Army Record of London* journal. 'The comic side of the situation was not lost on the men of the destroyer. The commander hailed the crew with a brusque invitation to surrender.'

For the *UC-5*, ze war was over, but moments before they obeyed orders to abandon their vessel, a member of the crew attempted to blow the vessel to kingdom come and deny the *Firedrake* the satisfaction of taking the sub intact.

'It was an act of heroism on the part of a young officer that rendered the submarine capable of being brought in as a prize,' continued *The Naval and Army Record*. 'The officer went down in a diving suit and made the mines safe by detaching the detonators, afterward securing them in such a position that the salvers could work in comparative safety.'

There was still a gaping hole in the hull but it was successfully towed to a dry dock at Harwich for repair. It took two years to fix the damage (there was a war on) and in July 1918 *UC-5* was put on display in London to illustrate the superiority of the Royal Navy over its German Imperial Navy rivals. Those in the know kept very quiet about the fortuitous way in which the U-boat came to be captured.

Thousands of Londoners flocked to the river to see a fabled and feared U-boat and it was such a propaganda success that it was subsequently shipped over to the States, where the Americans cut it into three pieces and put it on display in Central Park. The brave officer who'd risked his life to ensure *UC-5* didn't shatter must have been livid.

CROSSING THE DIVIDE
1926

There are essentially two distinct forms of bridge building. One is when two disparate groups come together in an attempt to find common ground and allay mutual suspicion and mistrust. The other is, well, just building a bridge.

According to the Thames River Trust, there are at least 214 bridges that span the length of the river. Why they are unable to put an exact figure on it is a mystery but, suffice to say, that's a lot of bridges. They come in all shapes and sizes. Some are designed for pedestrians and road traffic alike, some for the exclusive use of those on foot, but all have their own story. Some of these are actually quite interesting.

We have, of course, already investigated the unfortunate history of the earlier incarnations of London Bridge (see 'London Bridge Falls Down') but the capital's other crossings also boast intriguing back stories.

For example, Waterloo Bridge is also referred to as the 'Ladies' Bridge', built predominantly as it was by the fairer sex while London's men-folk were fighting in the Second World War, whereas Vauxhall Bridge was the first crossing in the city to carry a tram over the river. The Albert Bridge earned the moniker 'The Trembling Lady' on account of its propensity to vibrate alarmingly under heavy footfall, especially when soldiers from the nearby Chelsea Barracks thumped their size nines down. To this day, a plaque still stands with the warning: 'All troops must break step when marching over this bridge'.

Further afield we have the Caversham Bridge, the Thames crossing in Berkshire between Caversham and Reading. Opened in 1926 by HRH the Prince of Wales, it was at the time the longest concrete bridge in the world with a span of 330 feet (100m).

Less imposing is the Bloomers Hole Footbridge in Oxfordshire, which is a steel skeleton clad in wood, and part of the Thames Path. It might not be much to look at but it joins its more glamorous cousins on this list as it needed a Chinook helicopter from RAF Brize Norton to lower its two 89-foot (27-m), 8-tonne central beams into place during construction in 2010.

The less said the better about the £18.2 million spent on building the Millennium Bridge (aka 'The Wobbly Bridge') in the capital and its subsequent two-year partial shutdown after pedestrians reported alarming movements of the structure.

WATER, WATER, EVERYWHERE

1928

The Thames is a fearsome force of nature and back in 1928 the river unleashed its full power with a flood of Biblical proportions that paralysed central London, killed 14 poor souls and left another 4,000 homeless as water cascaded through the capital's sodden streets.

The flood occurred on 7 January after heavy winter snow on the Cotswolds melted at the same time as a storm surge in the North Sea and an enormous spring tide, and the three uncontrollable meteorological factors combined to devastating effect.

The first part of the riverbank to burst was at Millbank opposite the Tate Gallery, damaging many valuable paintings. Westminster Hall, the House of Commons and various Underground stations were badly affected, while the Blackwall and Rotherhithe tunnels were also flooded. The capital had never seen anything like it and the river was measured 18 feet (5.5m) higher than it would be at a normal high tide, a full foot more than the previous record.

'To-day the amazing behaviour of the Thames did what nothing but a Lord Mayor's Show will do – populate the Embankment with a crowd,' reported the *Guardian* in the immediate aftermath of the disaster.

> This was when high tide was approaching. The slow crawling of the water, dark and menacing, up to about the level of the roadway was watched by thousands of people to whom the Thames had never been a spectacle before.

The warning of the Port of London Authority had stirred primitive terrors in the general mind, and people were staring at the river expecting its wild force to be released again.

All attempt at privacy was gone, and wherever a window was open, even on the ground floor, there would be a group of gazers exploring the poor pretence of a home with a sort of inquisitive sympathy. Here and there a woman would be grubbing about among a pile of broken and sopping furniture trying to redeem something, and sympathisers would be told how there had been no sleep since the flood came.

There was, however, one lighter note to the unwelcome event and that was the sight of the moat at the Tower of London filled with water for the first time in over 80 years.

The moat was originally dug in the 13th century in the reign of King Edward I but over the years it became more ornamental than a defensive necessity and by the 1840s it had become a deadly threat to the Tower's residents. The problem was that the toilets emptied directly into it and it became, according to the Tower's in-house doctor, 'impregnated with putrid animal and excrementitious matter, emitting a most prejudicial smell.' Which doesn't sound very nice at all.

Worse was to follow in 1841 when a cholera outbreak caused by the fetid moat water killed several of the soldiers billeted at the Tower and hospitalised 80 more, and it was wisely agreed that the moat had to be drained.

The work was finished in 1845 and the moat remained healthily dry for the next 83 years until, of course, a torrential Thames intervened.

LIFE IN THE SADDLE
1933

The Thames passes by scores of churches and graveyards as it makes its inexorable way from Gloucestershire to its rendezvous with the North Sea. There are unconfirmed reports of the river inadvertently sweeping away coffins after flooding but, on the whole, the dearly departed and the water coexist harmoniously.

Many famous people have found their final resting place by the banks of the Thames and one of the most intriguing and fascinating must be John Faulkner, a former jockey who is buried in the riverside graveyard of the church in Appleford-on-Thames in Oxfordshire.

To describe Faulkner's life as eventful would be an understatement. Born in London in 1829, he rode his first winner at the age of eight and was still in the saddle when other jockeys had long retired, riding professionally for the final time in a steeplechase at Abingdon at the grand old age of 74. To put that in context, 'Old John' (as he was affectionately known) was a maiden winner in the same year that Queen Victoria assumed the throne and was still in the saddle at Abingdon in 1903, two years after her death.

There was certainly pain to go with the gain during his evergreen career and he was once crushed between a train and a platform while attending to his horses. John, though, was made of strong stuff and despite all the inevitable injuries that came with life as a jockey, he lived to a ripe old age and finally joined the choir invisible at the age of 104 in 1933.

'John Faulkner, the world's oldest jockey, has died in Appleford, England,' reported one American newspaper on his death. 'It is claimed that he broke nearly every bone in his body during his career. He fractured a thigh two years ago [caused by a kick by a mule], and was bedridden until death. The change that has come over the status of the jockey is shown by his declaration that he received [just] six cents after riding his first winner at Epsom. He never made a bet in his life. "I have never believed in betting," he used to say.'

John apparently didn't believe in contraception either. Twice married, he was evidently a very 'loving' husband and fathered a staggering 32 children during his life, the last of his offspring arriving 39 years after the first.

'Old John' was buried near a big elm tree at the cemetery in Appleford, a stone's throw from 'Old Father Thames'.

THE GREAT CRAB GRAB
1935

Considering they are essentially the aquatic cousins of spiders, crabs are a surprisingly popular creature. Kids love to hunt for them in rock pools on idyllic summer holidays at the beach while adults are rather partial to a claw or two, washed down with a nice glass of Sauvignon Blanc or Chianti.

Yet not everyone is enamoured with our eight-legged (the claws don't count) marine friends, and some of the most vocal members of the anti-crab league are those who are concerned that one particular species is having a disastrous impact on the Thames.

The offending fella in question is the Chinese mitten crab, so called because the furry filaments on its claws (they're not legs, remember) make it appear as though it's wearing gloves. That's as cute as it gets, however, and there are real concerns mittens are decimating the banks of the river.

Native to Southeast Asia, mittens were first spotted in the Thames in 1935 and are classed as an invasive species, thought to have arrived in the UK as stowaways on Chinese boats. The problem is they have a tendency to burrow into riverbanks, creating boltholes from the strong currents of major waterways, and these cavities in turn cause erosion and collapse. Marine biologists estimate there can be as many as 28 burrows per square metre of bank.

The freshwater mitten's crimes do not stop there. A voracious predator, they've been steadily nibbling away at the Thames' resident worm and shellfish populations and have also been known to clog up water-intake pipes of power stations.

A thorough pest then and increasingly a nuisance as their numbers have grown in recent decades...but there could be a solution. Yes, we could eat the blighters. A study by Natural History Museum scientists in 2009 concluded the crabs were safe to consume and, although large-scale farming has yet to begin, we could be set to follow the lead of the Chinese, who consider mittens something of a delicacy. There has even been talk of exporting our unloved, rapacious mittens back to China in time for tea.

Or we could follow the example of one Chinese entrepreneur who came up with the cunning plan of selling our hairy crabs from a vending machine at the main subway station in Nanjing in Jiangsu province in 2010. Stored at a chilly but not fatal 41°F (5°C) to keep the fellas sleepy, and encased in a plastic straitjacket to keep them securely in place, the idea was an instant hit, with more than 100 mittens sold every day.

A Chinese mitten crab vending machine on the platform at Tottenham Court Road? It's our ecological duty.

GOING THE EXTRA
FOURTEEN MILES
1937

The debate over how long a piece of string really is has raged for centuries, fascinating and dividing philosophers and yo-yo makers alike. In contrast, readers who remember the introduction to this book will be aware there is no such confusion or controversy about the length of the River Thames, flowing as it does for 215 serene miles (346km) from Gloucestershire to the North Sea.

Or at least that's what certain maps would have us believe – but it transpires that determining the true length of the river is not an exact science and in the past has even been the subject of heated Parliamentary debate.

Academics have been haggling over the mileage for years. The Ordnance Survey map shows the official source of the Thames at Thames Head, near the village of Kemble in the Cotswolds, about five miles southwest of Cirencester. If you accept that, the river is indeed 215 miles (346km) from start to finish. Job done, home time.

However, there are those – some would call them heretics – who insist that the source is in fact at Seven Springs, four miles (6.4km) south of Cheltenham. Seven Springs is the source of the River Churn, which flows into the Thames at Cricklade, and, they argue vociferously, you'd have to be insane not to understand the logic. Intriguingly, if you're in the Seven Springs camp, it adds 14 miles (22.5km) to the length of the Thames and would make it nine miles (14.5km) longer than the River Severn.

The two rival sources each have a stone plaque to champion their claims. 'This stone was placed here to mark the source of the River Thames', reads the predictable epitaph at Thames Head, while the inscription at Seven Springs reads, *'Hic Tuus O Tamesine Pater*

Septemceminus Fons'. Which is obviously the Latin for 'Here, O Father Thames, is your sevenfold source.' A score draw on the plaque front then.

In February 1937, the debate reached the dizzy heights of the Houses of Parliament when two Gloucestershire MPs began something of a war of words on the thorny subject. The two protagonists were Sir Walter Robert Dempster Perkins, the Conservative MP for Stroud, and William Morrison, the Conservative chap for Cirencester and Tewkesbury.

Perkins kicked off the war of words by demanding the next edition of the Ordnance Survey map identify Seven Springs (yep, slap bang in the middle of his constituency) as the true source of the river.

'I understand that it is not an invariable rule in geographical practice to regard as the source of a large river the source of the tributary most distant from its estuary,' replied Morrison. 'I am advised that the source of the Thames or Isis is the spring known as "Thames Head", and that the leading authorities agree that the name of the stream which rises at Seven Springs is the "Churn". In these circumstances it does not appear that the alteration suggested would be justified.'

'Is the Right Honourable Gentleman aware that the source known as Thames Head periodically dries up as in 1935,' replied Perkins. 'And is he also aware that the source known as Seven Springs is twice as high above sea level as the source known as Thames Head, as well as being farther from the estuary?'

'I am aware of these considerations,' conceded Morrison, 'but they do not alter my view, as confirmed, that the River Thames rises in my constituency and not in that of my Honourable Friend.'

Unfortunately for Perkins, Morrison also happened to be the Minister of Agriculture and Fisheries at the time of their spat and he was jolly well going to use his influence in Cabinet to ensure Thames Head was not usurped. The OS maps did not change and to this day still show Thames Head as the aquatic cradle of the river.

You, of course, are entitled to side with either camp, but if you are poised, say, to take a Geography GCSE, stick with 215 miles.

AMY'S MYSTERIOUS DEMISE

1941

The Second World War tragically claimed millions of lives during six years of brutal fighting but one of the most high-profile casualties of the conflict was the famed pilot Amy Johnson, a victim of a doomed flight in aid of the war effort which remains shrouded in mystery and confusion.

Amy became a household name in the 1930s as she indomitably set a sequence of flying records. The first female pilot to fly solo from England to Australia, she was also the first to fly from London to Moscow in a single day and set a new record for the fastest flight from London to Cape Town. Johnson was the undisputed queen of the skies.

When war broke out, she was not allowed to fly combat missions but she put her skills to patriotic use in the Air Transport Auxiliary (ATA), ferrying planes across the country for the RAF, and it was on one such seemingly routine ATA mission that Amy met her premature end.

She set off on the morning of 5 January 1941 from Blackpool destined for RAF Kidlington, Oxford, but veered 100 miles (160km) off course and reportedly ran out of fuel and was forced to bail out over the Thames Estuary. Despite the efforts of the crew of HMS *Haslemere*, who had seen her parachute from her plane, they were unable to rescue her. The *Haslemere*'s brave captain, Lt Cmdr Walter Fletcher, lost his own life attempting the rescue and a nation mourned the loss of its flying heroine.

Her body was never recovered from the Thames. The official report blamed adverse conditions (thick freezing fog) for Amy's death but what really happened that day is a question that is yet to be satisfactorily answered. For years some speculated that Amy was not on a simple transport assignment but rather flying her German lover out of the country. Others argued she was shot down by the Luftwaffe, while the conspiracy theorists suggested she faked her own death.

In 1999, however, the plot thickened when Tom Mitchell, an anti-aircraft gunner stationed on the banks of the Thames Estuary in 1941, came forward with a startling claim.

'Amy was shot down because she gave the wrong colour of the day [a signal to identify aircraft known by all British forces] over radio,' Mitchell revealed. 'Sixteen rounds of shells were fired and the plane dived into the Thames Estuary. We all thought it was an enemy plane until the next day when we read the papers and discovered it was Amy. The officers told us never to tell anyone what happened.'

There has never been an official response to this version of events but the story took an even more dramatic and grisly turn in 2002 when a former RAF clerk called Derek Roberts was interviewed by the BBC's *Inside Out* programme. One of Roberts' friends, Corporal Bill Hall, was on the *Haslemere* that fateful day and the two had met shortly after the failed rescue attempt.

'He came in to report what had happened,' Roberts told the BBC.

I took down what he said. I typed the report and he approved it and I put it to the flight commander. He came in with the crew that were landing and he was a bit shaken. He said that while he was on deck, a parachutist had come down in the water and had drifted near the *Haslemere*. She called out that she was Amy Johnson, that the water was bitterly cold and could they get her out as soon as possible. They threw her a rope but she couldn't get hold of it.

Then someone dashed up to the bridge and reversed the ship's engines, as result of which, she was drawn into the propeller and chopped to pieces. Later on in life he used to say that there had been an official cover-up of Amy's death, that for some reason it had all been kept quiet.

It would have certainly done nothing for national morale to learn of such a gruesome event and, while the truth of her final moments remains contested, her record-breaking achievements in life are a legacy that cannot be questioned.

A TICKING
TIME BOMB
1944

The legacy of the Second World War was as far-reaching as it was bloody. Western Europe clung on to democracy, Hitler got his just deserts, America underlined its credentials as a superpower and Winston Churchill almost single-handedly kept France's champagne and brandy makers in business.

The six-year conflict also carelessly left rather a lot of unexploded bombs all over the place and one of the biggest, most ominous caches of ordnance can be found in the Thames Estuary, a huge stash of munitions that is still on board the sunken SS *Richard Montgomery*. The American ship was built in Florida in 1943 and the following year made the trip across the Atlantic laden with vital supplies for the Allied war effort, including 1,400 tonnes of assorted bombs and explosives.

The *Montgomery* made it safely to Blighty in late summer 1944 and, under orders to join a convoy heading across the Channel to Cherbourg, looked for a place to drop anchor. The local harbour master sent instructions to head to the Nore, the point where the Thames meets the North Sea, and wait. Disaster struck, however, on 20 August when the ship ran aground on a sandbank. As the tide retreated, the *Montgomery* broke up and is now permanently stranded in the shallow water. Even at high tide, the ship's three masts are still visible.

It's been nearly 70 years since the sinking but the dangers of its potentially lethal cargo have hardly diminished. According to a BBC news report back in 1970, an explosion on the *Montgomery* could throw up a 1,000ft-wide (300-m) column of water and generate a sixteen-foot-high(5-m) wave. In 2004 the *New Scientist* magazine concluded that a blast on the wreck would produce one of the biggest non-nuclear explosions ever seen and would devastate the nearby town of Sheerness, causing an estimated £1billion of damage.

The *Montgomery* is cordoned off by warning buoys to prevent other ships accidently ploughing into the wreck and it is monitored by the coastguard on behalf of the Department of Transport, but the big question is whether the ordnance can be safely disposed of.

'There's always been this debate, "Why not just blow it up and see what happens?" because the water would act as a denting mechanism,' said marine survey expert Ian Biles. 'But I can understand why they have adopted the approach they have to leave it alone. It's unknown territory.'

Previous attempts to decommission sunken ships from the Second World War have not exactly gone according to plan. In 1967, a salvage company tried to move munitions from a Polish ship that also went down in 1944 but triggered a massive explosion, the seismic ripples of which were detected 5,000 miles (8,000km) away.

The thorny issue of the *Montgomery* was brought back into focus in 2013 when London Mayor Boris Johnson confirmed proposals to build a new four-runway hub on an artificial island in the Thames Estuary. The only flaw in the cunning plan to expand the capital's airport capacity is that 'Boris Island' would only be a few miles from our ticking time bomb. Tourists might expect a few errant bombs in Kabul or Baghdad but it's not really the image London wants to present to the wider world.

'The population has lived with the wreck all these years and now the problem is brought into focus because of the airport,' said local historian Colin Harvey, the director of a film about the wreck worryingly entitled *Disaster Waiting to Happen*. 'The thinking is that if they build the airport then maybe they will deal with the wreck. It's going to have to be dealt with and the sooner the better.'

Understandably, there has been a conspicuous lack of volunteers to get the job done.

THE MYSTERY MONSTER
1956

We have already learned that the Thames is no stranger to alleged sightings of strange, frightening creatures (see 'Beasts of the Thames') and the tale of the 'four great fysshes' that were spotted lurking in the river back in 1457 was undoubtedly a cracker, even if they were eventually identified as 'two whales, a swordfish and a walrus' and promptly turned into sushi.

It was harder, however, to explain away the demonic-looking beast that swam up the river in 1956, sending Londoners fleeing in panic and foreign journalists into a feeding frenzy. 'The sea monster was first spotted in the river off Central London, Sunday,' wrote the correspondent from the *Ottawa Citizen* newspaper in February. 'It was going up the river. One man said it had an enormous dorsal fin and another claimed it had "big red eyes". People who saw it told police it was about five feet [1.5m] in length. Ripples around it gave the impression of a 35-foot-long [10.6m] body.'

Jeepers creepers. The mystery monster was later seen near Henley-on-Thames and the UK's finest marine biologists were absolutely stumped.

The fear lingered for days but terror quickly turned to embarrassment and then anger when it emerged our beast was in fact the handiwork of three Reading University students who were trying to drum up publicity for their Rag Day. Everyone had been duped but our mischievous undergraduates certainly caught the attention of the media, appearing in a March issue of *Time* magazine to show off their 'model' monster.

It is far from the only Thames-themed animal hoax. In 2006, *The Sun* reported a sighting of a penguin on the river, a long, long way from its Antarctic home.

It is believed to be the first time a penguin has been spotted in the Thames and comes weeks after tragic Wally the Whale got stranded. Experts said the penguin, normally seen at the South Pole, may have been released into UK waters by fishermen who accidentally snared him. Marine biologist Lil Faroop said: 'It looks like a Jackass. They feed on sprats and fly through the water at five miles per hour. They have a donkey-like bray.'

Unsurprisingly the story was published on 1 April, a date that still failed to alert some members of the government, who called for the aforementioned penguin to be repatriated because it didn't have a valid visa.

There was also a deluge of sightings of the Loch Ness Monster in the Thames in 2003 although, to be fair, it wasn't an elaborate hoax but rather a floating model to promote tourism in the Scottish Highlands, presumably in lieu of Nessie actually making a verified appearance in the lake itself.

WINSTON'S FINAL FAREWELL
1965

It was in 2002 that the BBC's *100 Greatest Britons* programme anointed Winston Leonard Spencer-Churchill as the nation's most cherished, most significant and most influential figure after a nationwide poll that saw the former prime minister fend off challenges from the likes of William Shakespeare, Charles Darwin and Isambard Kingdom Brunel.

It was, in truth, no great surprise. Defeating Hitler and the Nazis, successfully defending European democracy and enjoying the odd drink or five go a long way to endearing a chap to an otherwise fickle British public.

Churchill joined the choir invisible in 1965. Surprisingly for a man famed for his dubious diet and seemingly incessant imbibing, he lived to the ripe old age of 90 but when news of his death broke, the country went into mourning and planning for a state funeral befitting a national hero began in earnest. It was an event that would rewrite the funereal record books and in which the Thames would play a central role.

By decree of Queen Elizabeth II, Winston's body lay in state in Westminster Hall for three days. Following that his lead-lined coffin was transferred to a boat called the *Havengore* and on 30 January the vessel made its solemn journey along the Thames from Tower Pier to Festival Pier ahead of the funeral service at St Paul's.

After business was concluded in the cathedral the coffin was taken to Waterloo Station, respectfully loaded onto a specially painted carriage and carried by rail to Hanborough Station near Oxford and finally to the graveyard of St Martin's Church in Bladon, where, as per his wishes, Churchill was buried in the family plot.

Thousands lined the side of the tracks to pay their last respects as the train made its journey from the capital to Oxfordshire but it was the sheer scale of the day's sad events that makes it noteworthy; for a man who made such a profound impression on the country via the radio during the Second World War, it was ironic that Winston's funeral was the television event of the era.

An estimated 350 million people worldwide (or one in ten of the global population) watched as the *Havengore* carried the coffin along the Thames. In Europe only Ireland declined to broadcast live coverage of the funeral and 25 million Britons unable to attend the event in person are believed to have tuned in to witness Winston's farewell. It was a staggering reflection of the man's enduring legacy in the UK and beyond, and the largest state funeral the world had seen at that time.

An interesting footnote to the story is the fate of the *Havengore*. Built in the 1950s by Tough's Boatyard in Teddington, the same firm Churchill commissioned to make boats used in the Dunkirk evacuation during the war, the 87-foot (26.5-m) barge is still in operation today after being restored in the 1990s.

It was part of the 40th-anniversary procession on the Thames to mark Churchill's death in 2005, as well as the pageant held to mark the 200th anniversary of the Battle of Trafalgar the same year, and is now available for family services and the scattering of ashes on the river.

A LITTLE PIECE
OF AMERICA
1965

The water meadow known as Runnymede, running along the banks of the Thames 20 miles (32km) west of London, is legendary as the place where King John sealed the Magna Carta in 1215. Unfortunately John then rather unsealed the deal with his disgruntled barons when he ripped up the document as soon as their backs were turned, but Runnymede nonetheless is now famous for its role in English democracy, as well as the look of disgust on the king's face when he was compelled to sign on the dotted line.

What is less well known about Runnymede is that two acres of the historic area actually belongs to the United States of America.

The unlikely land grab was instigated in the wake of the assassination of John F. Kennedy in Dallas in November 1963. With America in shock and mourning, an appeal was launched to raise funds to build a permanent memorial to JFK in the UK and Runnymede was selected as the site for the final monument, a tablet of Portland stone in a memorial garden inscribed with a quote from his famous Inaugural Address in Washington in 1961.

'Let every Nation know,' it reads, 'whether it wishes us well or ill, that we shall pay any price, bear any burden, meet any hardship, support any friend, oppose any foe to assure the survival and the success of liberty.'

The icing on the cake, though, was the decision to gift the memorial garden site to the people of the United States (it has since been transferred to the ownership of the federal government) and JFK's widow Jackie flew to London in 1965 and jointly dedicated the memorial with Queen Elizabeth II in May.

Which all means that, should you be sailing down the Thames past Runnymede, you are technically drifting past a small and rather remote outpost of the United States, which manages to make Hawaii look local.

A RIVER
HOLIDAY
1967

The British are rather partial to caravanning. There are an estimated one million caravans in the UK (although mercifully not on the road all at the same time) and, according to the RAC website, 'celebrity caravan owners include Robbie Williams, Jeremy Vine, Dame Kelly Holmes, singer Jay Kay and actor Steve McFadden, who plays Phil Mitchell in *EastEnders*'.

And if you become a member of the Caravan Club, a snip at only £43 per year, you can even enjoy 'huge savings on everything from the M6 toll and restaurant meals to show tickets'. You'd have to be mad not to sign up.

Caravan technology is, of course, constantly evolving and in the 1960s the last word in mobile holidaying had to be the 'Creighton Gull', the world's first (and possibly last) ever amphibious caravan. Jesus could walk on water but with a Creighton Gull, you could actually holiday on the stuff.

Built by the Creighton Caravans company near Nelson, Lancashire, the Gull looked like any other caravan on the road but once you unleashed her on the water she was transformed into an elegant boat complete with outboard motor. It was the invention the world had been waiting for but Creighton Caravans needed to get their message out and in 1967 they gave the Gull a public test drive. They chose a stretch of the Thames near Henley for the big launch and invited the cameras of British Pathé to capture the moment.

'Some people like messing about on boats, others prefer caravanning,' enthused the reporter despatched to witness the Gull in action for the first time. 'Well now they can do both in the same vehicle. It's got four berths, including the captain's cabin. The driver

– or is it helmsman? – can forget the worries of the road as he cruises down the river. At about £760 anyone can be king of the river or the roads. Comes in quite useful in the rainy season too.'

Sadly the caravanning community were not quite as impressed as our waggish reporter. Despite healthy initial orders, spiralling costs and slow manufacturing times made turning a profit on the Gull impossible, and only two years after it was unveiled Creighton Caravans ceased production.

You can enjoy the black-and-white Pathé footage of the Gull on the Thames online, a poignant reminder of British ingenuity and idiocy in perfect balance.

THE PHANTOM HITCHHIKER
1972

London is reputedly awash with ghosts. Judging by the myriad myths and alleged sightings (not to mention the lucrative ghost walk business), the capital seems to be groaning under the weight of paranormal activity. If you've been to the Big Smoke and not seen something supernatural, you've been robbed.

The Thames' entry in the prestigious and highly competitive 'best ghost story' category belongs to the Blackwall Tunnel, which runs beneath the river between Greenwich and Tower Hamlets, and the strange, albeit completely unproven, tale of the disappearing hitchhiker.

The legend has it that in 1972 a motorcyclist was approaching the south entrance of the north tunnel. At the entrance he spotted a hitchhiker wearing biker's leathers and, seemingly touched by a sense of motorcycling fraternity, he decided to give the stranded man a lift. He asked to go to Leigh-on-Sea in Essex, hopped onto the back of the bike, the engine roared into life and the pair sped through the Blackwall Tunnel towards Tower Hamlets.

When they emerged from the darkness, our big-hearted rider turned around and realised his passenger had vanished. Fearing the hitchhiker had fallen off in the tunnel and got himself crushed by an HGV, he quickly turned the bike around but could find no trace of the mystery man beneath the river.

Our motorcyclist was an inquisitive soul and the following day he rode out to the address in Essex he'd been given by the hitchhiker. A man matching the description had indeed lived at the house, he was told, but, you've guessed it, he'd died 12 years earlier. His premature death was, wait for it, a result of a fatal motorbike crash at the entrance of the Blackwall Tunnel.

Our 1972 encounter is not the only report of a phantom hitchhiker unnerving travellers through the tunnel but it is certainly the most chilling. The details of our spooky story have diverged with the retelling over the years – history's version of Chinese whispers – but the narrative is essentially the same and a timely reminder that there are dangers, earthly or otherwise, in picking up hitchhikers.

FATHER FIGURE
1974

No one can be certain when 'Old Father Thames', the mythical and benign personification of the river, was brought to life. He may now be ubiquitous in the folklore of the river, featuring in countless poems, songs and paintings, but his exact origins have sadly been lost in the fog of history.

It is reassuring, though, to know Father Thames is still around to keep a paternal eye on the water and all those associated with it, and if you happen to be passing through St John's Lock near Lechlade, Gloucestershire, you cannot miss a rather fetching stone statue of the man himself, reclining leisurely as he looks out across the river.

'The long-haired figure with a flowing beard reclines by barrels,' writes Ron Emmons in his book *Walks Along the Thames Path*, 'which represent the cargo once carried on the river. He also holds a spade, which represents the digging of locks to make the river navigable.'

The statue, however, was never intended to reside at St John's. Created by the Italian sculptor Rafaelle Monti, the Portland cement effigy was first put on public display at the Great Exhibition in 1851. There it remained for 85 years but when the Crystal Palace burned down in late 1936, 'Old Father Thames' had to be dramatically rescued from the flames.

The statue became the responsibility of the now defunct Thames Conservancy group and in 1958 they rehomed it at Thames Head, the traditional source of the river. Unfortunately, 'Old Father' didn't enjoy his new residence and after a series of attacks by vandals he was moved to St John's Lock in 1974, safe from the attentions of mindless idiots.

The St John's Lock effigy is not the only Thames statue in existence. There is a similar statue, sculpted by John Bacon, in

Richmond Terrace Gardens which was purchased by the Duke of Montagu in 1781 for 100 guineas and, like its cousin, has suffered the indignities of vandalism and is now missing one of its arms.

Another 'Old Father Thames' made an appearance at Limehouse in East London in 2013 when a nine-foot (2.7-m) figure mounted on a 20-foot (6-m) plinth was unveiled on the river's shoreline. The Limehouse Father's celebrity credentials were certainly impeccable, fashioned by sculptor Antony Gormley, the man behind the *Angel of the North*, and sold to the actor Sir Ian McKellen, who owns a pub in the area. The statue gives the impression of walking on water at high tide, a trick that many *Lord of the Rings* devotees believe Sir Ian can also pull off.

ANARCHY ABOARD
THE *QUEEN ELIZABETH*
1977

The first floating concert to grace the Thames was the historic performance of Handel's classic Water Music back in 1717 (see 'A Very Royal Musical') but exactly 260 years later the river witnessed an altogether more riotous gig which hit the headlines for all the wrong reasons.

It was 1977 and the Queen's Silver Jubilee. Most of the country was celebrating but not everyone was putting up the bunting and anti-Establishment sentiment was embodied by a popular beat combo by the name of the Sex Pistols. Loyal monarchists, the boys were not.

The band of course had made a controversial name for themselves with the release of their infamous single 'God Save the Queen' but in the summer of 1977 their music was banned by the BBC and the boys were not allowed to perform on English soil. The Pistols' manager Malcolm McLaren, however, had a cunning idea. How about hiring a London barge called the *Queen Elizabeth*, sailing down the Thames, knocking out a few tunes at the height of the Jubilee euphoria and metaphorically sticking two fingers up at the Establishment? The river, after all, wasn't technically English *soil*.

On 6 June the boat set sail with the Pistols and their entourage on board. They performed 'Anarchy in the UK' as they glided past the Houses of Parliament but as the drink flowed the party got more raucous and the barge's captain radioed the police for help. The boat pulled into dock where the boys in blue were waiting in numbers and McLaren reportedly ran screaming down the gangplank to confront the long arm of the law.

'The police took him to one side,' recalled journalist Tony Parsons, who was on the boat, 'and gave him the worst beating I've ever seen anybody given.'

The concert was the talk of the town and, although it had been brought to an abrupt halt, it undoubtedly generated the publicity that McLaren had yearned for.

'The band had done nothing wrong,' said Richard Branson, the boss of the band's record label Virgin. 'Nobody had done anything wrong but the very act of raiding the boat and then about 12 policemen physically beating up Malcolm McLaren with truncheons obviously propelled the Sex Pistols onto the front pages of all the papers.'

The Sex Pistols' 'victory', however, was short-lived. Seven months after tearing up the Thames the band had acrimoniously split while, at the time of going to press, HRH was still very much on the throne.

To rub salt into the wound, 'God Save the Queen' was rereleased in 2012 to coincide with Her Majesty's Diamond Jubilee but only made it to No. 80 in the charts. Which all goes to prove that you mess with the Royal Family at your peril.

DOCKERS THREATEN DISASTER

1982

Union militancy was blamed for many of the ills of Britain during the 1980s. It was invariably Prime Minister Margaret Thatcher angrily pointing the finger of blame at the likes of Arthur Scargill, and the PM made it her personal mission to destroy the powers of what she famously described as the 'enemy within'.

Many still revile Maggie for her one-woman war but had they known how perilously close dockworkers came to condemning parts of southern England to catastrophic flooding from the Thames, they may have been less sympathetic to the union cause.

The year was 1982 and work on the Thames Flood Barrier was almost complete. All that was left to do was fit the all-important 300-tonne gates in place and London could breathe easy, safe in the knowledge the capital was now safe from the threat of flooding. The problem was the gates were stranded in the Northeast due to an industrial dispute over pay between the dock workers and the Tees and Hartlepool Port Authority. To make matters worse, the banks of the Thames in Kent and Essex had already been raised in readiness for the higher water levels once the barrier was working and flood season was fast approaching. If there was a flood before the gates were fitted, it would be funnelled straight into central London.

'A severe London flood is probably the most damaging natural disaster liable to affect these islands,' the prime minister was warned in a confidential memo from the Department of the Environment, released in 2013 under the 30-year rule. Casualties would be 'numbered in hundreds rather than dozens', it added.

Maggie had a big problem and such was the threat that the

government even considered a controversial solution that would condemn Kent and Essex to a watery fate in a bid to spare the capital. The memo continued:

> If all else fails it might be necessary to provide that, if a major surge of water was threatened, the flood defences downstream would be breached so that some of the water would flood low-lying land in Essex and Kent rather than central London.

> There is a major political difficulty in that the Government would have to take responsibility for deliberately flooding Kent and Essex in order to protect central London. [If London floods] the water will be polluted because of the flooding of sewers. There will be widespread electricity failure, structural damage to roads, bridges and buildings and earth slippage resulting in fractured sewers and gas and water mains. There is also a risk of looting and other outbreaks of civil disorder.

Crikey. The gates had to reach London sharpish and Maggie resolved that the dockers' strike had to be broken. Not for the first time, she got her way and by December 1982, the Thames Flood Barrier was fully operational. The residents of Kent and Essex were, of course, blissfully unaware how close they had come to being condemned as the capital's sacrificial lambs.

SHUTTLE SERVICE

1983

Nestled on the banks of an embryonic River Thames in Gloucestershire, not much normally happens in the sleepy village of Kempsford. The annual village fete is apparently a humdinger but for the rest of the year excitement can be in decidedly short supply for the 1,200 residents.

The month of May 1983 was an exception to the rule. All initially seemed reassuringly tranquil but then there was a roar from the clouds and as if from nowhere the American space shuttle *Enterprise* loomed into view, flying above the village. You could have knocked the vicar over with a feather.

To be accurate, *Enterprise* was not actually doing the flying. It was in fact strapped to the back of a modified Boeing 747 but it did make a startling appearance over Kempsford that day before touching down at RAF Fairford, an American air base on the outskirts of the village and just a few hundred metres from the Thames.

The story of how a rural Gloucestershire spot came onto NASA's radar began in 1943 when RAF Fairford was built during the Second World War. Seven years later, at the chilly height of the Cold War, we handed control over to our friends across the Atlantic for use as a strategic bomber base and, of course, being American, they had to make the runway bigger and better. They ended up extending it to a whopping 3,000 metres (nearly 10,000ft) long.

When the shuttle came into service in 1981 NASA needed a number of emergency landing sites across the world in case there were problems in the minutes immediately after lift-off, and Fairford's elongated runway ticked all the boxes, becoming the UK's only 'TransOceanic Abort Landing Site'. If the shuttle took off but couldn't make orbit, Fairford offered sanctuary.

From 1981 to 2011, Fairford was on standby every time there was a shuttle launch planned from the Kennedy Space Center, although it was thankfully never called upon to save the day. The final *Atlantis* shuttle flight in July 2011 passed without incident and Fairford was stood down.

'I suppose I'm sad,' admitted airfield manager Tony Maycock in the build-up to Atlantis' swan song. 'I've been here for 10 years and we've been on standby for that time. We hope we never see it, but this is the last time we hope we never see it.'

So what of *Enterprise*'s touchdown by the banks of the Thames back in 1983? That was merely a scheduled refuelling stop for the jumbo jet as it piggybacked its famous passenger to the Paris Air Show, but at least Kempsford did get one fleeting glimpse of the shuttle before it was mothballed.

PRESCOTT'S
POLITICAL PROTEST
1983

John Prescott has always been, well, a larger-than-life political figure and during his entertaining career as an MP wherever he went, comedy and controversy loyally followed. His 'finest' hour, of course, came in 2001 when he decided the best way to win the general election was to punch a voter, but Prezza ensured he was never far from the headlines with his amorous, extramarital activities and his dubious decision to get the public purse to pay for two new toilet seats for chez Prescott.

The Member of Parliament for Hull East always had a certain gift for self-publicity and back in 1983 Prezza burst onto the nation's TV screens when he undertook a mile-long swim of the Thames in protest at the Conservative Government's policy of dumping nuclear waste at sea.

The stunt was preceded by John appearing on breakfast show *TV-am* for a chat with Nick Owen, and the country nearly choked on its cornflakes when Prescott waddled into the studio almost bursting out of a frogman's suit. What he expected to encounter in the river that necessitated the big knife ostentatiously strapped to his left leg was a mystery.

'We want to get across to the people of this country that we're poisoning our seas,' Prezza preached from the sofa. 'I think if I get that home to the people I will have achieved something. We must stop it. When a mother takes the little children in the summer to the beaches and they paddle in the sea, shouldn't she be assured that we're not having radiation being emitted into the sea and causing cancerous problems?'

It wasn't exactly the kind of PR the English Tourist Board were hoping for but subtlety was never Prezza's forte and he duly ploughed down the river to make his point. Subsequent reports of a stranded whale in the Thames were the work of cruel wags.

The year before Prescott's public dip a fella by the name of Alex Allan windsurfed past the House of Commons en route to his office at HM Treasury, another bizarre example of the political elite using the Thames for a bit of self-aggrandisement. Allan went on to become Tony Blair's Internet Czar, the British High Commissioner for Australia and the head of the Joint Intelligence Committee, but back in 1982 he was vexed by how to get into work with a London rail strike on.

His colleagues sensibly opted for taxis or the bus but Allan rejected such mundane solutions and hopped on his windsurfer, sporting a pin-stripe suit, bowler hat, umbrella and leather attaché case. Mercifully, the incredible show-off got exactly what he deserved when he pulled level with Big Ben – a gust of wind took hold of his sail and he was thrown into the river.

WINNIE'S LEGACY
1984

Pooh sticks is the epitome of sporting simplicity. Find a stick, locate a convenient bridge and drop your wood in the water. Job well and truly done. There's no need for expensive equipment, the training regime is very relaxed and the coaching manual brief.

The exact origins of pooh sticks are hotly disputed. Some believe the game was created by *Winnie the Pooh* author A. A. Milne and his son Christopher as they played by the River Medway in East Sussex, with Milne then committing it to paper in the 1920s. Others insist pooh sticks was only brought to life *after* Milne penned his *The House at Pooh Corner* story and it was only after the book was published that the game became a reality.

Unfortunately, not even Christopher Robin Milne himself can remember the exact sequence of events. 'It is difficult to say which came first,' he admitted in his autobiography *The Enchanted Places*.

> Did I do something and did my father then write a story around it? Or was it the other way about, and did the story come first?

> But in the end it was all the same. The stories became a part of our lives; we lived them, thought them, spoke them. And so, possibly before, but certainly after that particular story, we used to stand on Pooh Sticks Bridge throwing sticks into the water and watching them float away out of sight until they re-emerged on the other side.

We do know that since 1984 a stretch of the Thames in Oxfordshire has proudly played host to the annual World Pooh Sticks Championships, an event that attracts competitors from as far afield as Japan and Australia and proof that even in our electronic age, the simplest of pastimes can enjoy enduring popularity.

Staged each year at Day's Lock near Dorchester-on-Thames, the championships were the brainchild of former lock-keeper Lynn David, who got the idea after watching walkers enjoying impromptu games of pooh sticks. Lynn decided to hold an annual contest to raise funds for the RNLI and the World Pooh Sticks Championships was born.

There are, according to the *The Official Pooh Corner Rules for Playing Pooh Sticks*, two golden rules. All the other competitors must agree to your choice of stick before battle can commence and you must drop and never, ever throw your stick into the water. Life bans are threatened for those who ignore either.

More than 1,000 people now descend on Day's Lock for the event and it has also been making waves in the media world. Four-year-old Aidan Eltham, the 2012 individual champion, appeared on BBC's *One Show* after his triumph, Chris Evans has talked about the championships on his Radio Two breakfast show and it was voted 'Britain's Favourite Quirky Event' by *Countryfile Magazine*.

Praise indeed, but disaster almost struck in 2013 when an Environment Agency flood alert in March on the Dorchester stretch of the Thames briefly threatened to bring to an end 30 consecutive years of the event – but organisers simply postponed it and staged the championships in October. Told you pooh sticks was simple.

LETTER FROM BEYOND
THE GRAVE
1999

'I hope that someone gets my,' sang the Police, 'I hope that someone gets my, I hope that someone gets my message in a bottle, message in a bottle.' Sting perhaps could have put it more pithily but you get the general idea. Stories of the discovery of letters sealed in bottles are, of course, relatively common but few, if any, can rival the amazing tale of Essex fisherman Steve Gowan and the startling catch he inadvertently made back in 1999.

Steve was minding his own business, angling for cod in the Thames Estuary, when he accidentally hooked something. On closer inspection he realised it was an old, green ginger-beer bottle and, after wiping away years of accumulated mud, he could see there was paper inside. He opened the screw-on rubber stopper and found a covering note.

'Sir or madam,' it read, 'youth or maid, Would you kindly forward the enclosed letter and earn the blessing of a poor British soldier on his way to the front this ninth day of September, 1914. Signed Private T. Hughes, Second Durham Light Infantry. Third Army Corp Expeditionary Force.'

The bottle and its contents had improbably survived in the Thames for 85 years and the search for Private Hughes' family began. Sadly it transpired that the man himself had been killed just two days after penning his message, but Steve was able to track down his daughter, 86-year-old Emily Crowhurst, to Auckland and flew out courtesy of a complimentary ticket from the New Zealand Post Office to deliver the letter in person.

It read: 'Dear Wife, I am writing this note on this boat and dropping it just to see if it will reach you. If it does, sign this envelope on the right hand bottom corner where it says receipt. Put the date and hour of receipt and your name where it says signature and look after it well. Ta ta sweet, for the present. Your Hubby.'

Despite having much of the world's media suddenly descend on her home uninvited to cover the remarkable story, Emily was understandably delighted to receive her father's emotional message in a bottle. 'It is hard to believe,' she said. 'It has been overwhelming. It touches me very deeply to know that his passage reached a goal. I think he would be very proud it had been delivered. He was a very caring man.'

WHEEL OF MISFORTUNE
1999

One of London's most iconic tourist attractions, the London Eye stands at an imposing 443 feet (135m) tall on the south bank of the Thames, an architectural masterpiece which has only served to strengthen the river's worldwide reputation.

You'd think the Thames would be grateful but when the Eye was under construction in 1999 and engineers were frantically trying to get the job finished in time for the capital's eagerly anticipated Millennium celebrations, the river actually conspired against it.

Things were already behind schedule. The central wheel was lifted into place a month late after cables became loose and construction workers then had to down tools when environmental activists broke through security, climbed the structure and spent the night chained to it in protest against dam projects in India and Spain. What on earth that had to do with the Eye is a mystery but the clock was now ticking ominously.

And then in October the Thames threw its own spanner in the works. The wheel's 32 passenger pods, built by a French ski-lift company, were finally en route to London from Grenoble. The final leg of their journey was along the river by barge and engineers initially breathed a collective sigh of relief when they caught sight of the first two pods, each weighing in at nine tonnes, sailing up the Thames.

They were due to dock opposite the Houses of Parliament but only got as far as Tower Bridge, halted by a high tide that made it unsafe to attempt to pass underneath. The pods were stuck and, as the BBC's Robert Hall was quick to point out, the Eye 'simply cannot afford any more hitches'.

The widespread panic on site receded, however, when one bright spark pointed out that a high tide has a tendency to become a low tide and all they had to do was wait for nature to take its course. The level of the river obligingly dipped after a few hours and the pods finally made it safely to their destination.

The next two months witnessed a flurry of activity to get everything done but, come New Year's Eve, everything was all right on the night. The London Eye (née The British Airways Millennium Wheel) was officially opened by Tony Blair, who in a very real sense cut the ribbon, and although the public weren't actually allowed on until March the following year, the capital had its new revolving attraction.

THE REAL BRAIN DRAIN
2001

Headaches are, by definition, a real pain but at least modern sufferers can reach for that fabled panacea that is Nurofen and whisper a silent thank you to the miracle of pharmaceutical technology. There are few minor ailments that a couple of painkillers cannot cure.

Sadly, our forefathers (and foremothers) were not so lucky. Medicine was far more rudimentary back in those days and one skeletal discovery in the Thames in 2001 provided a stark reminder that, despite its faults and failings, we should all be frightfully grateful for the NHS.

The find was a Bronze Age skull of a man. Skulls dredged from the river are hardly a rarity but this particular specimen, discovered near Chelsea, dated back to 1750 BC and displayed one particularly alarming feature – a gaping hole in the bone. The result of a painful mishap with a sword, perhaps? An injury sustained from a well-aimed spear during a scuffle? Maybe the man had taken simply a nasty tumble?

Apparently not. Experts examined the skull and concluded the circular gap in the bone structure was actually the result of the ancient surgical procedure of trepanning, a process in which a hole was drilled or cut in the skull to expose the fleshy interior. It was a surgery designed to relieve a wide range of health and intracranial problems and, lest we forget, was conducted without the benefit of any namby-pamby modern anaesthetics or painkillers. You had to be seriously ill or mad to agree to undergo trepanning.

Remarkably, the skull bone showed signs of having grown back following what must have been the excruciating surgery, suggesting our man survived his ordeal. The hole itself was also surprisingly neat, indicating the bone was carefully scraped away rather than simply gouged or sawed as was the way in Continental Europe.

'Trepanning is probably the oldest form of surgery we know,' explained Dr Simon Mays of English Heritage. 'The skull shows that there were people in Britain at the time with significant anatomical and surgical skills, ones not bettered in Europe until Classical Greek and Roman times more than a thousand years later.'

Interestingly, although 40 other trepanned skulls had previously been found in the UK, our 2001 discovery was the first unearthed in the London stretch of the Thames, begging the question whether Bronze Age Londoners were generally healthier than the rest of the country or were simply more reluctant to let some quack take a sharp knife to their skulls.

DIVE, DIVE, DIVE!
2001

Diving may be the scourge of modern football but it's also jolly good fun to don a wetsuit, flippers and mask and explore the natural wonders of an underwater world that is normally hidden from us. The majority of divers take to the water for the sheer pleasure of it but the two sub-aqua interlopers who took a dip in the Thames in 2001 had more nefarious motivations for getting wet.

Our miscreant divers were swimming one evening by the side of a cargo ship freshly arrived from Jamaica, moored near the Thames Barrier, when they were abruptly intercepted by a police speedboat and hauled out of the water. The pair claimed they were merely members of the recently formed 'Thames Nocturnal Diving Club' but the Old Bill weren't born yesterday and slapped on the cuffs.

A closer inspection of the ship revealed £2.5 million worth of cannabis strapped to the hull in waterproof containers and the boys in blue leaped to the quite reasonable conclusion that the divers were attempting to retrieve the drugs. They were charged with conspiracy to supply a Class B drug and got six and four years' porridge respectively. It was, fact fans, the first time in legal history divers had been arrested in British waters trying to recover a stash of smuggled narcotics.

'The operational team were faced with immense logistical problems,' said Detective Superintendent Barry Phillips. 'I would like to praise the operational team leaders and in particular the crews and the gun boats who faced a perilous task operating on the Thames in complete darkness.'

In the wake of the successful operation, 24/7 covert surveillance was rolled out on all of the Thames legitimate diving clubs but the payback was disappointing, resulting in one meagre caution for the illegal resale of discarded Tesco trolleys.

FOWL PLAY
2001

The Thames is home to myriad duck species but you'd probably be surprised just how many of the yellow rubber variety have made an appearance on the river over the years, abandoning their natural habitat of the family bathroom and going for a swim on the wild side.

There were 60 of the bright-yellow blighters let loose on the water in 2001, for example, when the Thames Water Parliamentary Duck Race was staged, a bizarre event which saw MPs and members of the Greater London Authority gather on Westminster Bridge to race their replica yellow ducks over a 500-metre course.

A PR stunt designed to highlight the increasing cleanliness of the river, the race was won by Tessa Jowell, the Secretary of State for Culture, Media and Sport, who refused to disclose her winning tactics after her triumph.

'There is not much skill involved,' said a Thames Water spokesman, immediately dispelling the sense of mystery. 'You just throw the duck in and it's first past the post.'

In the summer of 2006 the Thames was awash once again with toy ducks but this time they arrived in serious numbers when 20,000 of them, inexplicably wearing sunglasses, were spotted bobbing about in the water all in the name of charity. Part of a fundraising event dubbed the Great London Duck Race beginning at Battersea Park, the race was almost ruined when the tide swept half of the contestants out of their specially roped off channel, but plucky Duck #335 was unperturbed, winning in an impressive time of 30 minutes.

It was size rather than weight of numbers, however, that made the most recent replica-duck incursion on the river in 2012 so spectacular, a 50-foot-high (15m) monster which began its eye-catching journey at West India Dock.

Weighing a whopping half-tonne and towed by a tugboat, the enormous yellow bird – part of an initiative to make people smile more – was so big Tower Bridge had to be opened to let it through and thousands of Londoners and tourists alike stood transfixed as it glided through the capital.

There were fears the duck could be vandalised when it finally came to a halt next to HMS *Belfast* but luckily it escaped any fowl play.

HICKS' HEROICS
2001

Jet-skiing down the Thames in central London is a daunting prospect in anyone's book. The plethora of pleasure boats, the river's many ferries and cargo barges, not to mention the stone and metal foundations of the umpteen bridges, all present a formidable set of obstacles and just one slip of the steering wheel could be disastrous.

Imagine, then, making the same journey without the sense of either sight or hearing. It's impossible, isn't it? Well actually not, as proven by deaf and blind jet-skier Graham Hicks on his remarkable jaunt down the Thames in 2001 without a scratch to either body or machine.

Nicknamed 'G-Force' on account of his boundary-pushing exploits, and an employee of the charity Deafblind UK, Graham took to the river after a challenge from a chap called Jon Hartland, who was a big cheese at Sainsbury's. The task was to get from Peterborough to London in a 'unique' way and our Graham wasn't going to disappoint. He set off from Sainsbury's HQ in Peterborough – delivering Mr Hartland his pound of PR flesh – on a tandem but decided to complete the final push to the capital on a jet-ski, reasoning that arriving in a black cab wouldn't quite cut it.

Graham successfully navigated down the river without hitting Tower Bridge thanks to a hearing and sighted pillion rider who communicated directions to him through a touch-based signalling system, completing his amazing trip at Blackfriars.

Sainsbury's had to stump up £7,000 for charity for all the 'free' publicity. 'I never expected him to do something as spectacular as making his way by tandem and jet-ski but that's Graham for you,' said Hartland. 'He's fired with adrenalin and he's determined to prove to the world that deafblind people can achieve as much if not more than able-bodied people, given the opportunity.'

Graham, however, was already contemplating his next challenge. 'If any other company wants to set me a challenge,' he said, 'then I'm open to suggestions.' Tesco were on the phone within minutes.

FAYED FUNNY BACKFIRES
2002

Whatever your view on Mohamed al Fayed, you've got to admit the fugger's got a sense of humour. His stand-up routine about the Royal Family is comedy gold and the statue he commissioned of Michael Jackson and inexplicably plonked outside Craven Cottage was hilarious. He's a funny boy, our Mohamed.

In 2002, however, al Fayed surpassed himself when, on Sunday 31 March, he announced on his website that he intended to float his iconic Harrods store. The press release promised more details the following day and with the London Stock Market poised to open in a few short hours, everyone was jolly excited. On Monday morning, al Fayed revealed the true extent of his comedy genius. 'What more appropriate place to float the world's most famous store,' sniggered our waggish Egyptian shopkeeper, 'than on the world's best-known river, the River Thames?'

Geddit? Despite it being 1 April, some people didn't and al Fayed had to issue a further clarification that both announcements were 'intended for amusement only'. Harrods would neither be floating on the stock market nor the Thames. Stop it, Mohamed, you're killing us.

This, however, is not the end of the bizarre tale and it's safe to assume the smile was rapidly wiped off al Fayed's face when he became embroiled in a bitter legal wrangle with American publisher Dow Jones and the *Wall Street Journal* as a result of his Thames-themed tomfoolery.

The *Wall Street Journal* initially failed to realise the story was a joke and ran it in the paper. There were red faces all round in the news room when they realised their mistake and a few days later they ran a second piece which compared Harrods to Enron, the American company notorious for a multi-billion-dollar fraud scandal.

Mohamed was not amused. The lawyers were unleashed, ordered to pursue a claim for defamation, and a lengthy legal battle ensued. The judge urged both parties to try and find a 'sensible compromise' to their problem but al Fayed hadn't got where he is today by backing down and the row rumbled on.

It was finally resolved in February 2004 when another judge ruled that Dow Jones was not guilty of libel after lawyers for the *Journal* pointed out the 'Enron' story had been read just 12 times by online readers from the UK and that a mere 10 copies of the newspaper were sent to British subscribers.

It was game, set and match to Dow Jones. Al Fayed walked off muttering something about Prince Philip nobbling the judge and in 2010 he flogged Harrods to Qatar for £1.5 billion. Harrods remains firmly in Knightsbridge rather than on the Thames.

THE LIFEBOAT DELIVERY
2002

One of the many claims to fame that marks out the Thames as anything but your run-of-the-mill river is the fact it boasts its own lifeboat service. No other inland waterway in England can say the same and should you be unfortunate enough to take a tumble into the Thames anywhere between Teddington and the North Sea, you can expect one of the service's E-class Tiger Marine boats, capable of speeds of 40 knots, to be there to save the day within 15 minutes of your impromptu dip. Set up jointly by the Maritime and Coastguard Agency, the RNLI and the Port of London Authority, the new service was rolled out in January 2002 after a £2 million investment and since then the boats have dutifully patrolled the river.

Its mission statement, of course, is to save lives, but just a few months after its launch one of the lifeboats found itself in the business of bringing new life into the world, answering a 999 call from an expectant mother marooned on a houseboat.

The dramatic SOS came from Sunna Wathen, who was suddenly ready for the arrival of her baby. The problem was getting the midwives and their equipment to her in time, so rather than risk becoming ensnared in the London traffic, the decision was taken to deploy a lifeboat. The midwives were hurriedly picked up at Tower Pier and ferried the short distance to Butler's Wharf, where Sunna was breathing increasingly heavily.

They were nearly there but getting the midwives and their equipment to Sunna proved problematic and, after a quick conflab, the crew decided to carry them in through a large porthole in the side of the houseboat.

'The tide was low so we put the bow of the lifeboat on to the shore,' explained helmsman Stuart Richardson. 'Then we had to piggyback the midwives one at a time onto the shoulders of crewman Kevin Maynard. It was probably just as strange a delivery for them as it was for us.'

Thankfully the drama was finally over and Sunna safely gave birth to a healthy girl.

Five years later there was another baby girl born on the river but this time the delivery was caught on camera. It wasn't, though, one of those excruciating birth films that some new parents insist on torturing friends and family with but a scene from Australian soap opera *Neighbours* in which the Izzy Hoyland character goes into labour during a wedding on a cruise boat, thus following the golden soap rule that babies must be born in increasingly improbable locations and never, ever in a hospital.

PAPERING OVER THE CRACKS
2003

Water is the sworn enemy of paper. Even a drop of the wet stuff can instantly disfigure a pristine piece of A4, and anyone who has dropped a tenner in a puddle or spilled Evian on their newspaper is acutely aware there's usually only one winner when H_2O comes into contact with parchment.

And yet, just occasionally, paper does beat rock, scissors and even water, and 2003 witnessed one such moment when comedian-cum-adventurer Tim Fitzhigham paddled down the Thames in a kayak made from paper. There was, in truth, some glue and waterproof resin also involved but paper was definitely the main building material.

Fitzhigham was aiming to break a 384-year-old record set by a fella called John Taylor for the longest distance covered on the Thames in a paper vessel. What first possessed Mr Taylor to attempt such an idiotic feat back in 1619 is a complete mystery, but ours is not to reason why and, for the record, he managed to travel 40 miles (64.4km), embarking from the City of London before sinking at Queenborough on the Isle of Sheppey.

Fitzhigham fared considerably better. Setting off from Lechlade in Gloucestershire in his kayak, he successfully made it all the way to Tower Bridge without his craft becoming a saturated, sodden mess, a total distance of 160 miles (257.5km).

'We have done 160 miles and the boat is still looking good,' said Fitzhigham as he gratefully climbed back on terra firma. 'I can't believe it. It has got a couple of bits of gaffer tape and a bit of sogginess on the port side, but she's really doing well. We really have beaten the record – we've smashed it. The waves were a bit bigger than I thought they might be and there were a couple of moments when I almost went under.'

Fitzhigham subsequently turned his experiences on the river into a comedy show *Paper Boat,* which he took on a nationwide tour.

Launching home-made vessels onto the Thames can have its pitfalls as one student discovered in 2005 when he tried to travel down the river on a boat made from rubbish. Remarkably our scholar from the Chelsea Art College had not just blown his tuition fees in the union bar. He was, it transpired, trying to sail down to Margate in order to jump on a ferry en route to his native Germany and decided a craft cunningly constructed from empty fizzy drinks bottles, discarded tubing and lashings of gaffer tape would be just what the doctor ordered.

He got about 200 yards before a bemused passer-by spotted he was in trouble and called the Port of London Authority.

'We intercepted him just off the Millennium Dome,' said a spokesman. 'We strongly advised him that he was putting himself and others in danger. He left the river but the following day he was seen again on the foreshore near the Isle of Dogs. He said he wanted to sail to Margate and then take a ferry to France and reach his home in Berlin. When he was asked why, he replied, "It is all part of a project of mine".'

The mystery Teutonic mariner was spotted at 11 in the morning on that second day, amazing bystanders who had never before seen a student out and about before midday.

YOU CAN LEAD A HORSE TO WATER

2004

Seahorses are curious, complicated creatures. As a member of the fish family, they are surprisingly poor swimmers. They boast a chameleon-like ability to change colour to mimic their surroundings and they use their snouts like vacuums. Then there's the male seahorse's bizarre acquiescence in giving birth to the next generation. Mrs Seahorse definitely wears the trousers in that relationship.

You would of course be forgiven for thinking *Hippocampus* (that's Latin, folks) is an oceanic beast. The clue is in the name, but recently our strange-looking friends have increasingly been making a home in the Thames, adding an exotic splash of colour to the river's marine ecosystem.

Seahorses were once a familiar sight in the Thames but pollution inevitably weaved its devastating magic and by 1976 it seemed the last seahorse in the river had sadly bought the farm. There were no sightings of the little fellas for 28 years but in 2004 a fisherman in the Thames Estuary hauled up his net and discovered what he initially thought was an ex-seahorse.

'At first he thought it was dead,' said David Knapp from Southend's Sealife Adventure Centre, where our little friend was eventually homed. 'He put it in a bucket of water and when he looked at it again it was swimming around quite happily.'

Seahorses generally prefer the warmer waters around the Bay of Biscay and the Channel Islands, making the colder waters of the Thames an unlikely habitat, but our solitary *Hippocampus* proved to be merely the vanguard of a larger repopulation and in 2008 colonies of the rare short-snouted seahorse were found further upriver at Dagenham in East London.

It was a strangely well-timed discovery. The new colony was located on a Monday, just 24 hours after seahorses became a protected species under the 1981 Wildlife and Countryside Act. It was almost as if they'd been patiently waiting for their new legal status to come into effect before deigning to show themselves.

'These amazing creatures have been found in the Thames on a number of occasions in the last 18 months during our regular wildlife monitoring work,' said London Zoo's Alison Shaw. 'It demonstrates that the Thames is becoming a sustainable bio-diverse habitat for aquatic life. It is not clear how endangered short-snouted seahorses are because there is little data known, particularly in the UK, so every scrap of information is valuable.'

No one knows exactly how many seahorses now call the river home but if Mr Seahorse is upholding his part of the marital bargain, the Thames could be teeming with them.

MALCOLM'S MARVELLOUS MARATHON
2004

Endurance rowers are a rare – some might argue masochistic – breed, instinctively drawn to the water to test sinew and technique, and the greater the aquatic challenge the better. The long stretches of the Thames are, of course, simply irresistible and, for years, oarsmen and women have been battling to set new and ever more exhausting records on the river.

One of the most daunting challenges is the journey from Lechlade in Gloucestershire to Southend Pier, a 187-mile (301km) slog, which most people would only dream of undertaking with the aid of an outboard motor, pre-booked hotels en route and a steady supply of sandwiches.

An attempt to scull the route in 2004 by a three-man team from Bedford Rowing Club in a high-sided, coxed double scull designed to cope with the narrow stretches of the upper Thames, as well as the rougher conditions in the tidal estuary, came to a premature end due to bad weather conditions, but just six days later a six-man crew from Dittons Skiff and Punting Club did complete the course in a new record time.

The team, which featured 1976 Olympic silver medallist Mike Hart, used a traditional Thames rowing skiff and came home in a time of 30 hours, 57 minutes and 20 seconds, eclipsing the previous record of 38 hours and 43 minutes, which had been set by members of the Lower Thames Rowing Club back in 1993.

Individuals also embark on similar challenges and in 2005 it was Malcolm Knight who set himself the exacting target of rowing a 165-mile (266km) route from Lechlade Bridge to Gravesend Pier as quickly as possible. At 51 years old, Malcolm was no spring chicken but had previous when it came to rowing records with the fastest time for a solo scull across the English Channel. Perhaps it should have come as little surprise that he glided over the finishing line in 43 hours, 40 minutes and 56 seconds, smashing the previous record by a staggering 10 hours. It is estimated he made 38,000 strokes of his oars during his river marathon.

'It took me three or four days to get back into a normal sleeping pattern and well over six weeks for any sort of recovery to occur but it was totally worthwhile,' he admitted.

> It is very fulfilling to have achieved my target by such a margin. It is fantastic and I am very proud.
>
> There are 44 locks on the way along the Thames so I stopped at each of them briefly for a stretch and something to eat, but I cut out the major rest periods. Psychologically it was easier to break the distance down into thinking about reaching the next lock. If you think about the whole thing it makes it very difficult. My family and friends thought I was completely bonkers.

They're not the only ones, Malcolm.

YOU CANNOT
BE SERIOUS
2004

There are sound, practical reasons why tennis is a sport traditionally played on dry land. Introduce a watery element and the balls would get distinctly soggy, spectators would have to remortgage their homes to enjoy a bowl of strawberries and cream and we wouldn't be able to tell whether Andy Murray was crying or not. It's why the lovingly manicured grass of Wimbledon in SW19 is a reassuring two miles from the banks of the Thames.

Which is also why commuters on their way to work in London one summer's morning in 2004 were understandably surprised to see John McEnroe enjoying a hit with Monica Seles on the river, a strange case of tennis abandoning its heartland in search of a new, albeit bemused, audience.

McEnroe, the three-time Wimbledon men's champion, and Seles, the 1992 women's runner-up, served and volleyed their merry way down the river from the London Eye to Tower Bridge on a specially adapted barge as part of a publicity stunt for a rather rapid credit card from the States, and it certainly made a novel change from the Boat Race in terms of a Thames-based sporting occasion.

'It was such a thrill to play with John on a barge on the Thames,' said Seles. 'I have never done anything even close to this before. I am thinking this was a dream. I've had some nervous moments in my career but sea legs is a new one for me.'

The barge's final destination was a mooring close to Tower Bridge where the great unwashed could grab a racket, hit a few forehands and no doubt switch their credit card allegiance to a provider with highly competitive rates.

The stunt was, on balance, a PR success but almost ended in acrimony when Seles smashed a backhand long into the river and demanded McEnroe retrieve the ball. There are absolutely no prizes for guessing his indignant reply.

A DRAMATIC SPARK
2005

Electricity bills are one of the banes of modern life. Those cursed numbers on the meter seem to spin around faster than an agitated fruit machine and the day the dreaded bill inexorably forces its way through the letterbox is about as welcome as Kate Moss at a Weight Watchers meeting.

In the old days, of course, power was cheaper. In fact, if you had the ingenuity and money to build a water mill by the banks of the Thames, you could happily use the river's considerable natural force for absolutely nothing; for centuries grain was ground, corn crushed and timber sawn without a three-pin socket or extension lead in sight.

One of the last working mills on the Thames could be found at Sonning Eye in Berkshire. It proudly resisted the onslaught of the modern, technological world until it reluctantly closed in 1969, but 13 years later it enjoyed a new lease of life when it was rebranded and reopened as the Mill at Sonning theatre.

A neat trick, but the electricity bills were giving the owners sleepless nights and in the early 2000s plans were hatched to harness the flow of the Thames once again, although this time around it was powering the theatre's footlights rather than making flour that was on the agenda.

An 18.5KW turbine capable of generating 162,000 units of electricity annually was installed, saving an estimated 75 tons of carbon dioxide each year, and in July 2005 the Mill at Sonning became the first theatre to be powered by Thames hydroelectricity. A deal was also put in place to sell any excess electricity produced back to the National Grid.

'It's a huge pipe in the river that has a siphonic action,' explained general manager David Vass. 'The tail part is six feet under the river.

The water, once it starts siphoning over, goes through a large pipe with a boat propeller inside. The water pressure turns on the propeller which drives the generator and that generates the electricity. The mill was always used for generating power [from] the 15th century onwards. We thought all this power is going underneath us every day and is being wasted, so we thought why not go back to the way it was in the old days and make good use of it.'

Sadly the Mill's artistic director declined to green-light a stage version of Seamus Heaney's book *Electric Light* to mark the illuminating occasion.

WHITE WATER
2005

The Thames has long been a liquid bin for London, uncomplainingly washing away the debris and detritus the capital no longer requires. The strain on the river has been dramatically reduced in the last century but over the years everything from body parts to abandoned cars, unloved bikes to unfortunate family pets, has been swept away by the power of the Thames.

The river usually keeps shtoom about the less palatable things it is forced to convey downstream but in 2005 it sang like a canary when a group of scientists decided the Thames might be acting as an unwitting drugs mule. Specifically, they suspected the river was awash with cocaine.

Commissioned by the *Sunday Telegraph*, the boffins arrived armed with their test tubes, white coats and safety goggles in search of evidence of Colombia's finest, taking various water samples along the length of the river. The chemical compounds of cocaine do not break down easily, even after passing through both user and into the sewage network, and the scientists were confident they could get an accurate picture of illicit drug use in the capital by carefully analysing the water.

What the Thames told them was startling. The results suggested a whopping two kilograms of cocaine were being inadvertently flushed into the river each and every day. That's the equivalent of 80,000 lines of the imported Class A drug every 24 hours, or just short of 3 million per year. Extrapolating their findings, the team reckoned a total of 250,000 Londoners must regularly be polishing off between them 150,000 lines of cocaine on a daily basis, 15 times more than previous official estimates from the government.

The news was greeted with dismay by health care experts and drug awareness groups but was less of a surprise to the Thames' more experienced anglers, accustomed as they had become to hooking the river's increasingly overexcited, wide-eyed fish.

PHARAOH FLOATS BY
2007

Ancient Egypt and the River Thames would not appear to have much in common. The Land of the Pharaohs immediately conjures up images of parched deserts and vast expanses of sand, while the Thames has an essentially wet quality about it.

But they say opposites attract and so it was in 2007 when weary London commuters on their way to work were suddenly confronted with the bizarre sight of a giant statue of Anubis, the jackal-headed Egyptian god of the dead, floating down the river. Standing an imposing 25 feet (7.6m) high and weighing in at nearly six tonnes, the black and gold fibreglass creation was certainly eye-catching as it made its way on the back of a cargo ship to Trafalgar Square.

Anubis, who, according to legend, protected the dead on their journey to the underworld, was not indulging in a spot of sightseeing but rather having a three-day stint in central London to promote the upcoming 'Tutankhamun and the Golden Age of the Pharaohs' exhibition, which was transferring across the Atlantic from Philadelphia to the Millennium Dome.

'That's really his role here today,' wibbled an excitable London tourism spokesman as Anubis glided down the Thames. 'He's protecting the Tutankhamun exhibition as it leaves America and heads for the UK.'

What Lord Nelson made of his new neighbour in Trafalgar Square is debatable.

Two years later the Thames experienced a second Egyptian invasion. This time it was a giant model of a pharaoh fashioned from 200,000 Lego bricks that sailed down the river. Although it stood at a more modest 16 feet (4.9m) high, it was still one hell of a sight.

The statue was on its way to Legoland Windsor in Berkshire, to form the centrepiece of the park's new £3 million 'Kingdom of the

Pharaohs'. It had taken a team of four Lego boffins over in the Czech Republic five months to build the impressive model, and after travelling the 1,395 miles (2,245km) from Eastern Europe by truck, it was decided to undertake the final leg of the journey on water, launching from the King George V Dock in East Ham.

It took the pharaoh 24 hours to make it to Windsor. The journey time could have been halved, of course, but the suits at Legoland were determined to squeeze every last drop of free publicity from the trip and ordered the skipper to keep the boat in first.

A LONG
JOURNEY'S END
2007

The Thames has served as the setting for the final leg of many an ambitious adventure or exciting expedition. A host of travellers have completed the last, arduous metres of their journey borne on the river into the heart of London, longing no doubt for a rapturous reception, a hot bath and a book deal.

None, though, can have been quite so relieved to lay eyes on the capital or quite as physically exhausted as Jason Lewis in 2007 when he navigated his custom-made, twenty-six-foot (8m) boat *Moksha* up the river and over Greenwich's meridian line at London's Royal Observatory. It was the end of a seriously long trip.

To be more precise, it was the climax of a 46,000-mile (74,000km), 13-year odyssey, which saw plucky Jason become the first person to circumnavigate the globe solely using human power. Some people will do absolutely anything to avoid flying budget.

Jason began his epic trip on the Thames in 1994 aged just 26 with the pedal-powered *Moksha* taking him across both the Atlantic and the Pacific. On land, he cycled, in-line skated and occasionally just walked. He was 40 by the time he finally returned to England but there were prolonged 'breaks' along the way as he paused to take odd jobs, including working on a cattle ranch in America and for an Australian funeral home, to fund his trip. He was also laid up for nine months in the States after he was knocked off his skates by an 82-year-old drunk driver, breaking both his legs. Getting arrested in Egypt on suspicion of spying or the crocodile attack he suffered but obviously survived off the Queensland coast probably weren't in his top five Kodak moments either.

'It feels fantastic,' Jason admitted as he stepped onto dry land.

I came over the line and I was choked. I blubbed like a baby. Everything I've been doing for the last 13 years has been in some way connected with this trip and tomorrow that will be no more.

There have been many high moments. To be honest, it's always good to reach the other side of an ocean. But if it was just about the physical challenge I would have got bored.

The 'why' question changed over the years. I started circumnavigating the world but it became more about using the expedition as an educational tool to enhance children's learning experience in the classroom.

Unsurprisingly, Jason did get the book deal and in 2012 *Dark Waters (The Expedition Trilogy, Book One)* was published. Hopefully, books two and three will not take as long as the journey itself.

DOGGY
PADDLE
2007

Raising money for good causes is a noble and altruistic act. Charities have benefited to the tune of millions and millions of pounds courtesy of the generosity of the selfless souls prepared to set themselves a challenge and help fund vital schemes for the disadvantaged, disabled or down on their luck.

The only problem is engaging with sponsors weary with yet another request for their cash. The answer is to devise ever more 'innovative' themes for fundraisers and these days you can't simply run the London Marathon or swim the Channel. You've got to have a shtick. Or a silly costume.

And so it was in 2007 when TV vet Joe Inglis, he of *Vets in Practice* and *Blue Peter* 'fame', decided to raise money for the Hearing Dogs for Deaf People charity. As a fully signed-up member of the showbiz fraternity, our Joe knew he needed to generate a bit of media interest and, after an arduous brainstorming session in the bath, he came up with the idea of rowing down the Thames in a giant dog bowl.

'I grew up by the river, so I've always enjoyed messing about in boats,' he explained. '[My pet dog] Jack loves swimming too, which could come in handy if we sink. The charity helps so many people and I hope that my Thames challenge will raise awareness of them and hopefully provide some funds.'

The dog bowl was cunningly fashioned from an old cattle trough, hilariously christened the 'Mutty Bark', and Joe and Jack set off in July from Cricklade, Wiltshire, heading for Putney some 150 miles (240km) downstream. Mercifully he didn't make a dog's dinner of it and, nine days after casting off, the dynamic duo made it safely to London.

'This was a challenge and I didn't think through the implications of rowing a round bowl,' Joe admitted. 'I fleetingly thought about rowing across the Channel but after nine days onboard, I decided against it.' Jack declined to share his thoughts on the unusual trip with reporters.

RUGBY REPLACED
BY ROWING
2007

Flooding is a bad thing. London can testify to that after the capital was dramatically swamped by the Thames in 1928 (see 'Water, Water, Everywhere') and anyone who wants to work for the Environment Agency learns on their first day that too much water in the wrong place is a definitive negative.

There are, though, exceptions to every rule and in 2007 the teachers and pupils at a school in Oxfordshire turned a sudden deluge to their advantage when the Thames burst its banks and submerged five of their rugby pitches in two feet of murky water. Egg chasing may have been off the syllabus for a while but sport did continue as the students took to the water in their boats, rowing happily across the temporary lake that had suddenly appeared in the school grounds.

'It happens every few years,' teacher Michael Edwards told the BBC. 'It's a good way of getting some practice in. You actually get waves on the water, especially if the winds get up. The river is just too fast and too dangerous for them to practise on at the moment.'

Not all the Henley-on-Thames school's budding rowers were able to reap the benefits of the flood. 'It's not challenging enough for the older ones training for the Henley Regatta,' Edwards explained.

The school certainly has something of a rowing pedigree. 'We have a successful club that is located on the banks of the River Thames just upstream from the world-famous Henley stretch,' boasts the school website.

There are around 100 members in the club who compete in races throughout the season. We also have extensive facilities including numerous ergometers or rowing machines, a weights room and two Boat Houses containing an excellent fleet of boats.

In Year 9 the boys start off by rowing with two oars; this is known as sculling. The main aim for this year is to learn the basics of rowing and boys usually row in Octuples and Quads. After Year 9 the transition is made to sweep rowing with one oar. At this stage most age groups will row in Eights.

The unscheduled flood of 2007 and the extra rowing practice it afforded evidently had a positive impact on the school's fortunes on the water as later in the year three of their crews won national titles.

And the name of this proud educational establishment? Shiplake College, would you believe? No? Well, it's true.

ONE HELL OF A WELS
2008

We have already made note of some of the invasive species that today call the Thames home. Chinese mitten crabs (see 'The Great Crab Grab') already have their many feet firmly under the table and while a widespread piranha invasion is terrifying but unlikely (see 'Fisherman's Nasty Bite'), the population of the great river is a constantly evolving smorgasbord of natives and marine immigrants.

Mercifully an uneasy alliance of the 94 species of fish indigenous to the Thames is yet to form an aquatic answer to UKIP.

The most muscular of the new kids on the block is, without doubt, the Wels catfish, a bruiser of a beast, which can grow up to 13 feet (4m) long and weigh in at an eye-watering 400lb (180kg). It's a fish you really don't want to get on the wrong side of.

Native to Eastern Europe, the Wels is believed to have been introduced to Blighty in 1864 by professional soldier Sir Stephen Lakeman while he was home on leave from a posting in Romania, and ever since the small number of beefy catfish that have made their way to the Thames have been bullying the locals.

In 2008, one such fish ended up on the end of Brett Ridley's line. The 28-year-old amateur angler was trying his luck in the Thames near Kingston when he suddenly felt a tug. He could have been forgiven for thinking he'd accidentally hooked an errant submarine but, after a titanic 45-minute struggle, he managed to drag a giant Wels onto the bank.

'I'd left a mate to get me some bait but when I got home from work he hadn't done it,' Brett explained after taking a hard-earned breather. 'All that I had in my bag was a tin of luncheon meat so I used that.'

It was a seriously big catch. The British record for a Wels stood at 62lb (28kg) set back in 2000 while the UK record for any fish caught in running waters was 64lb (29kg) after Georgina Ballantine managed to land a staggering salmon from the River Tay in Scotland in 1922.

Brett was poised to make history but his record-breaking attempt hit a significant snag when he popped his prize on the scales and they bottomed out, making an accurate and verifiable reading impossible. Brett's reaction is not fit for publication, but suffice to say he was a tad miffed.

He did have the foresight to take a picture of his behemoth before releasing it back into the Thames and many experts conceded it looked like a '65-pounder or more' but while the Wels that day was not the one that got away, the record certainly was.

DIVING FOR TREASURE
2008

Losing things is simply part of the human condition. The more things we accumulate in life, the greater the risk of mislaying them, and who among us can honestly say they've never endured a frantic, desperate scrabble to locate the car keys, that repossession letter from the bank or one of the kids. Britain managed to lose an entire empire, so we can all surely be forgiven for briefly misplacing the TV remote.

Most losses are trivial, fleeting matters but sometimes they are heartbreaking and it was a case of the latter in 2008 when 93-year-old Second World War veteran Charles Brown headed to the Thames to attend a reunion, take a cruise from Kingston to Weybridge and a trip down memory lane.

A survivor of the famous evacuation of Dunkirk in the summer of 1940, Mr Brown proudly made his way to the river with his war medals – including his OBE as well as Dunkirk and Normandy campaign medals – but as he boarded his boat with the aid of a walking frame, they slipped out of the breast pocket of his jacket and fell agonisingly into the murky water of the Thames.

Initial attempts to retrieve the medals with magnets failed and all seemed lost until members of the Thames RNLI heard about Charles' plight and decided to do something about it. Six days later frogmen were in the water near Kingston Bridge conducting a search and, despite the odds being stacked against them, they resurfaced clutching sunken treasure.

'I wasn't sure we'd find the medals because they had been down there all week and visibility from the silt was bad due to all the heavy rain recently,' said Malcolm Miatt, the operations manager at Teddington RNLI. 'However, our divers found them almost immediately. There was no drama.

'The medals are a bit muddy and dirty and we'd like to get them cleaned up. The old guy is a hero and truly deserved to get his medals back. The RNLI is delighted to have cheered him up.'

The good news was quickly relayed to Charles at his care home in Woking and he was soon back at the riverside to reclaim his cherished medals.

'I do get a bit emotional because these medals meant so much to me,' he admitted. 'I wasn't a celebrity, a pop singer or a cricketer, these medals were what I was proud of. I'm not going to be celebrating with cream cakes or anything like that, just having the medals back is enough for me.'

If the RNLI divers could find all the lost change and jewellery that has found its way into the Thames over the years as quickly as they did Charles' medals, they'd be millionaires.

A MANACLED DEMISE
2009

Handcuffs are the *de rigueur* form of restraint in modern law enforcement. TV cops love nothing more than 'slapping on the cuffs' after they've successfully cornered their criminal quarry and even the biggest, baddest crook is rendered powerless once the metal bracelets have clamped their restrictive grip.

Back in the 18th century, the authorities favoured an even more sturdy way to keep transgressors in check, slapping the infamous ball and chain on those who were deemed a menace to society. Houdini may have been able to escape from handcuffs with an ingeniously concealed hair clip but the only way out of the ball and chain was to cut yourself free.

This was exactly what Magwitch did in Charles Dickens' *Great Expectations*, coercing Pip into stealing him a file to make good his escape from a Thames prison hulk (see 'Felons Afloat') and remove the 'great iron on his leg', but if you didn't have the right tools at your disposal, you were in serious trouble. Judging by the grisly find of an intact 300-year-old ball and chain in the river in 2009, there may have been some unfortunate souls who paid with their lives for the lack of a hacksaw.

The discovery was made on the banks of the Thames near Rotherhithe. The river's thick black mud had almost perfectly preserved the iron shackles and when experts from the Museum of London took a closer look, they realised the lock on the ankle brace was still firmly fastened in place.

There were two possible explanations. Either the ball and chain had been accidentally lost in the river by a careless guard or a desperate prisoner had leaped into the water hoping to swim to freedom but drowned, the body and then the skeleton slipping slowly away after three centuries submerged in the Thames.

'Whether a real-life Magwitch freed himself from the "great iron on his leg",' said archaeologist Kate Sumnall, 'or perished in shackles, or whether this ball was simply discarded, we can never know.' She added that the high quality of the iron used for the ball and chain made it unlikely that it had simply been thrown away, fuelling the theory it was in fact evidence of a rather grisly death.

The find subsequently went on temporary display at the Museum of London Docklands but the exact fate of our apparently doomed felon remains unresolved.

TALE OF
THE TAPE
2009

The Bayeux Tapestry is a magnificent work of art which chronicles the Norman Conquest of England in the 11th century and, in the case of the unfortunate King Harold, graphically illustrates that when you hear someone shout, 'Watch out for that arrow,' it's probably prudent not to look up and reply, 'What arrow?'

Apparently the Bayeux Tapestry is an embroidered cloth and not actually a bona fide tapestry but that's academic because the pertinent point here is that it is only 230 feet (70m) long, making it a full 197 feet (60m) shorter than the lesser-known Thames Tapestry, a superb celebration of the river's history, architecture, industry and nature, and the impact it has on the communities along its route. Bayeux has the history but the Thames Tapestry has got it beaten hands-down lengthwise.

A joint project between the Millennium Tapestry Company and the Thames Heritage Trust, the idea for the artwork was hatched in 2009 and invitations were sent out to schools along the river to get involved, asking each one to produce a metre-square panel of stitching that reflected what the Thames meant to them. The sewing kits were dusted off and some 60,000 children from 130 schools began work on a 'specific stretch of river'.

Slowly but surely the individual schools completed their squares. By the summer of 2012, the separate pieces had been combined to create the final Thames Tapestry and it was put on display for the first time as a complete work during the London Olympics and Paralympics in a three-month stint at St Paul's Cathedral. An estimated 50,000 people witnessed the exhibition.

Sadly, the Thames Tapestry was to be only a fleeting triumph. After the St Paul's gig, the work was reduced back to its constituent parts and the individual panels returned to the schools, much to the collective relief of those across the English Channel connected to the Musée de la Tapisserie de Bayeux.

WATER WINGS
2011

Although their natural habitat is the vast expanses of the ocean, aircraft carriers are not averse to the occasional sojourn on the Thames. The military leviathans are admittedly a bit of a tight squeeze through the Thames Barrier but at least Tower Bridge can rise to the occasion.

Back in 2007, HMS *Ark Royal* sailed up the river and parked at Greenwich to mark the 25th anniversary of the end of the Falklands conflict, while helicopter carrier HMS *Ocean* was in town in 2012 as part of the security operation at the London Olympic Games. A year later, HMS *Illustrious* visited the Big Smoke to help commemorate the 70th anniversary of the climax of the Battle of the Atlantic.

Those high-profile visits generated plenty of media interest but what was less publicised was the fact that the world's first ever aircraft carrier had been quietly enjoying a muddy retirement on the Thames for decades before *Ark Royal* et al showed up. The vessel in question was a 'Seaplane Lighter', designed by the Thorneycroft company and built in Kent for the Royal Navy during the First World War. Measuring in at a mere 58 feet (17.7m) long, it was a minnow in comparison to its modern successors and capable of launching just one plane, but no one can take its place in the record books away.

The Seaplane Lighter was born in a bid to extend the Navy's reconnaissance range across the North Sea and aid vital monitoring of the German High Seas Fleet. It was towed behind a destroyer and, when the time came, was released with a seaplane on its specially adapted deck. The Lighter was then partially flooded to lower the boat in the water and the seaplane would float off and start up its engines. Compressed air would then pump out the water and the Lighter was reattached to its destroyer.

Only 50 were ever manufactured and after the War our Lighter, the *H21*, returned to Blighty and was pressed into service on the Thames as a cargo boat. It toiled away uncomplainingly until the 1960s but was then left to rust on the riverbank. Everybody forgot about the diminutive piece of history until 2011 when a maritime journalist spotted it poking out of the water and realised it was much more than just another wreck. The Lighter was rescued from the Thames and taken to the Fleet Air Arm Museum in Somerset for restoration.

'It's only tiny but it's this ship that led to the development of the massive modern aircraft carriers,' said a museum spokesman. 'It's the world's first aircraft carrier and at the time the *Ark Royal* is decommissioned, it's fitting it's being restored to its original state.'

The *Ark Royal* ended up being hacked to pieces at a Turkish scrap yard to make razor blades and tin cans while the *H21* is sitting pretty at the Fleet Air Arm Museum, proving the bigger they are, the harder they fall.

FISHERMAN'S NASTY BITE
2010

Pollution of the Thames used to mean even the most optimistic fisherman would be more likely to hook a discarded shopping trolley than actually land a fish, but the river has been getting cleaner and cleaner since the 1860s (see 'The Killer River') and these days its aquatic residents are thriving.

Anglers are now a common sight on its banks and the explosion in fish numbers has seen more successful catches than ever before. Some, however, have been alarmingly exotic.

In August 2010, Richard Salmon (yes, that's his real name) was trying his luck in Marlow, Buckinghamshire, opposite the famous Compleat Angler Hotel no less, when he got a bite. Mr Salmon (honestly, it's genuinely his name) was expecting to reel in his usual carp or pike and was somewhat stunned to find a 4-inch (10cm) piranha on the end of his hook. That's a flesh-eating piranha, native to the warm waters of South America.

'I didn't expect to come eye-to-eye with a piranha,' he admitted. 'I normally fish for pike so I'm used to dealing with sharp teeth. But it was very unnerving unhooking it. I took it home so I could prove to my pals I caught a piranha from the Thames.

'I caught it with the same rod, the same bait and in the same spot I've been fishing in all my life. It's only three to four inches long and, to an extent, I was a little wary and careful how I pulled it off the line but it could only get your finger in its mouth, not your hand.'

The catch caused quite a stir as experts speculated how the hell the lone piranha had found its way into the Thames. They concluded it must have been released from an aquarium and that the river was unlikely to be infested with more of the carnivorous critters. Tellingly, none of them volunteered to take a quick dip to prove the theory.

It was not, though, the first time a piranha had been found in – or, more accurately, on – the Thames. Back in 2004, workers for Thames Water were quietly going about their business on a boat near Dagenham when a dead piranha suddenly appeared from the sky and landed on the deck of the boat.

'It is definitely a red-bellied piranha but it would not survive in the low temperatures of the Thames,' said Paul Hale, the curator of the London Aquarium, after being asked to clear up the mystery. 'We imagine it was probably released and then floated to the surface where it was picked up by one of the hungry seagulls and deposited onto the boat.'

It is an offence to release non-native species into the Thames. It's sheer madness to give piranhas a chance of adapting to the cold water and making a new home over here.

RECORD-BREAKING REGATTA
2012

Whether Queen Elizabeth II ever enjoys a glass of Guinness after a hard day's waving, smiling and generally looking regal is a secret closely guarded by Buckingham Palace Perhaps she prefers a gin and Dubonnet as her late mother did or maybe she's a Stella Artois kind of girl. We're just not privy to that kind of information.

We do know, however, that HRH does have some undeniable connection to the black stuff, appearing as she does so remarkably frequently in the *Guinness World Records (GWR)*. If there's a royal record to be broken, you can bet the Queen has had a crack at the title.

At the last count, Liz was currently the longest-reigning female monarch. She's the oldest British monarch in history, surpassing the previous record of 82 years established by George III, and her image has adorned the coinage of at least 45 different countries, smashing the milestone of the 21 national coins her great-great-grandmother Queen Victoria graced. With an estimated personal fortune of £310 million, she's the current undisputed queen of bling and on 9 September 2015, she will eclipse Victoria's record of 63 years, seven months and three days as Britain's longest-serving monarch.

Quite the go-getter then, and in June 2012, HRH added another *GWR* record to her burgeoning collection when more than 1,000 vessels took to the Thames to take part in the Diamond Jubilee Pageant, a river extravaganza that you might just have heard about.

The pageant was certainly spectacular and although only 670 boats made it all the way from Hammersmith Bridge to Tower Bridge, thus covering a minimum distance of two miles (3.2km) and qualifying for the final *GWR* count, it was more than enough to eclipse the previous record for the largest maritime parade of 327 vessels in tandem set in Bremerhaven in Germany in April 2011.

When the Queen sets her sights on something, there's just no stopping her.

However, it's lucky that *GWR* officials do not consider historical contenders for such categories because even Liz's impressive flotilla pales in comparison to the 10,000 or so vessels that clogged the Thames in 1662 for another quintessentially royal occasion.

The date was 23 August and King Charles II was en route by boat to London with his new Portuguese bride, Catherine of Braganza, whom he had wed in Portsmouth in May. The capital's residents were eager to catch a glimpse of their new queen and as the newlyweds floated down the river they were joined by 10,000 vessels in a grand celebration of their nuptials that became known as 'Aqua Triumphalis'.

According to the diarist John Evelyn, it was 'the most magnificent Triumph ever floated on the Thames, considering the innumerable number of boates & Vessels, dressd and adornd with all imaginable Pomp; but above all, the Thrones, Arches, Pageants & other representations, stately barges of the Lord Mayor & Companies, with various Inventions, musique & Peales of Ordnance both from the vessels and shore.'

'Musique', maybe, but did Charles' pageant feature the London Philharmonic Orchestra playing the theme from James Bond? No, it did not.

MUDDY WATERS
2012

Armed with little more than their trusty metal detectors and hope, amateur historians are a plucky, indefatigable breed who often endure endless hours searching for artefacts only to dig up an old Coke can rather than a gold coin from the reign of Edward the Confessor. They do occasionally enjoy moments of triumph, unearthing a rare historical gem, but it's not an exact science and patience is the name of the game.

The Thames boasts its own, distinct gang of artefact hunters known as 'mudlarks', who regularly scour the river's banks at low tide in search of treasure and who can trace their history back over 200 years.

The original mudlarks were basically professional scavengers in late 17th-century London, making a hand-to-mouth living locating any detritus beside the Thames that could be sold, refashioned or reused. The muddy and polluted banks of the Thames made for a filthy and frequently hazardous workplace as the capital's sewers spewed their foul contents into the water.

In contrast the modern part-time mudlarks, licensed by the Port of London Authority, are all about uncovering the capital's long and rich history and can be spotted sweeping the banks of the river with their metal detectors whenever the water recedes. Over the years they have discovered countless coins, pottery, cutlery, the odd skeleton and jewellery, but 2012 brought arguably the most intriguing find when mudlark Regis Cursan unearthed what proved to be a Roman legionary's token for... well, there's no polite way of saying this – a brothel. Dating back almost 2,000 years, the saucy token was found near Putney Bridge. Smaller than a 10-pence piece and made from bronze, the disc featured on one side a man and woman in, ahem, a rather amorous embrace.

'The day I made the find it was a very low, early tide and raining heavily,' explained Regis. 'At first I thought it was a Roman coin, because of the thickness and diameter. When I rubbed the sand off the artefact the first thing I saw was the number on one side and what I thought was a goddess on the other. Little did I know at the time it was actually a rare Roman brothel token. To find something like that is a truly exciting find.'

Intriguingly, it was the first time such a token had been discovered in Britain. Many had already been found in mainland Europe, which does beg the question whether London-based legionnaires were less amorous than their Continental counterparts or simply more careful with their tokens.

ROOM WITH A RIVER VIEW
2012

Musicians draw their inspiration from a diverse and frequently bizarre smorgasbord of places. The Boomtown Rats came up with 'I Don't Like Mondays' after a fatal shooting at a US school, Dire Straits came up with the title of 'Money for Nothing' after a comment by a washing machine salesman, while American punk pop chanteuse Ke$ha apparently stares at her own breasts in search of musical creativity.

In 2012, however, British singer-songwriter Imogen Heap turned to the Thames for inspiration for her new single, decamping to the South Bank for what proved to be a surreal stint by the river. Heap located herself on the roof of the Queen Elizabeth Hall. More precisely, she took up temporary residence in 'A Room for London', a one-bedroom boat/art installation plonked on top of the building. It certainly gave her jolly good views of the river as she began penning her new tune.

The process also involved Heap finding out what the Thames meant to Londoners, but rather than actually go up and ask them, she installed a 'customised audio-visual egg-shaped listening chair' in the nearby Southbank Centre and invited innocent passers-by to spill the beans.

A convoluted process then, but the proof is in the pudding and Heap eventually came up with the new song 'You Know Where to Find Me', the structure of which she claimed was influenced by the river's tidal ebb and flow. The song sadly failed to trouble the charts but with lyrics like 'All things to mend with bite-size lifeboats, I'll fix your smashed-up head' it wasn't exactly a mainstream offering.

Heap, however, did rather spoil her Thames theme when it came to recording the piano parts of the song, abandoning her boat atop the Queen Elizabeth Hall and heading up to Edinburgh where she 'borrowed' the pianos of 13 fans who had invited her into their homes via the medium of Twitter.

For a more faithful musical tribute to the great river we must look to Ralph McTell (he of 'Streets of London' fame) and his little-known song 'Dear River Thames', a ditty that definitely has a more 'Thamesy' feel to it. 'Dear River Thames,' warbles Ralph, 'for the ride, I must confide, that you are my friend.' Bless.

SAFE HANDS' RODENT SURPRISE
2013

Retirement for a professional footballer can prove a mixed blessing. There are only so many hours that can be whiled away counting the noughts on their bank statements or buffing their fleet of luxury cars. Bereft of the cut and thrust of a regular kickabout, many players find themselves at something of a loose end once they've hung up their boots.

It was a dilemma faced by ex-England goalkeeper David Seaman when he decided to call it a day in 2004. Initially 'Safe Hands', as he was dubiously dubbed, was content with preening his trademark moustache but after opting for the clean-shaven look, he really needed something to fill his days and the former Arsenal star plumped for fishing, signing up as a member of the Thames Valley Angling Association.

All was well in Seaman's world until September 2013 when he headed down to the river near Marlow, unpacked his tackle and got the surprise of his life when he was suddenly confronted by a giant rat. He couldn't have been more shocked if England had reached the World Cup final which, let's face it, is pretty unlikely.

To be accurate, it wasn't actually a huge rat but a capybara, the largest rodent in the world, but since it's native to South America and can measure 4½ feet (137cm) in length and tip the scales at 150lb (68kg), Seaman's shock was fairly understandable.

'It was just sat there, not afraid of me, so I took out my phone and captured a few shots of it,' our retired custodian explained. 'I didn't have a clue what it was, but it was as big as a sheep and I thought if it were to have a go it would take me down.'

It emerged the capybara had become a familiar sight on that particular stretch of the Thames, even making an appearance at the Henley Regatta in July, having escaped from a nearby farm.

'We have daily bulletins,' said the farm owner, Lady Judi McAlpine.

> He has taken possession of the river between Cookham Dean and Marsh Lock. He is eating everyone's windfalls and is clearly happy as a capi can be. Except of course that he may now have noticed that there are no girls out there. Meanwhile, his wife waits patiently.

> There is no point in our catching him again. We don't cage our animals and he would just be over the fence and back to the river. We really believe he will be back when it gets colder. If he shows any signs of stress we will be there like a shot with our big net and apples. We will play it day by day. He does like human company and he has taken to sitting by fishermen at night, just watching the river with them.

Whether our lonely AWOL capybara was an Arsenal fan is merely idle speculation.

A POPULAR POLITICIAN
2013

It's been a tough time for Britain's Right 'Honourable' Members of Parliament in the last couple of decades. The *Guardian*'s exposé of the sorry business of cash-for-questions in 1994 was the first nail in the coffin and ever since our democratically elected MPs seem to have been doing their level best to further sully the reputation of the Commons with a sordid series of sex scandals and dubious financial dealings.

The *Daily Telegraph*'s scoop in 2009 about the abuse of the Parliamentary expenses system, duck house et al, merely served to strengthen the impression that our MPs were about as trustworthy as a fox in, well, a duck house.

It would, though, be unfair to suggest all those who frequent the Palace of Westminster are irredeemable cads and there was a rare example of Parliamentary gallantry in October 2013 when a quick-thinking MP by the name of Stephen Gilbert turned life-saver to help rescue a woman from the clutches of the Thames.

Mr Gilbert was attending an event on the riverside terrace of the Houses of Parliament when he glanced downwards and noticed what he believed was a body floating by – when the 'body' moved, he realised the woman was still alive. Luckily our heroic Liberal Democrat MP for St Austell and Newquay didn't waste a second, grabbed a lifebuoy and threw it in the water. The woman managed to grab hold, buying her precious extra time, and she was eventually rescued by a Thames lifeboat (see 'The Lifeboat Delivery') and then taken to hospital by the London Ambulance Service.

'What looked like a body just floated past,' said Gilbert after the drama. 'Then I saw that the person then moved and I followed them down the terrace. There are some lifebuoys on the terrace, I guess this is not the first time something like this has happened. I didn't expect for the person to move and then I didn't expect to have to react to get them a lifebuoy. She disappeared towards Westminster Pier and she was rescued near to that.'

A lucky escape indeed, and it would certainly be churlish and uncharitable to suggest Gilbert would have reacted any differently had he known the damsel in distress was not a registered voter in his constituency.

THE NAME'S CROCODILE, MR CROCODILE

2013

The tale of sharks beating their predatory path up the Thames is not actually an urban myth (see 'The Punctual Shark') and over the years there have also been various alarming sightings of that other fearsome submerged killer, the crocodile, lurking in the river. Or maybe alligators, it's hard to be absolutely certain.

The prospect of swarms of crocs populating the Thames is not a happy one and in February 2013 it seemed that the invasion had begun when eagle-eyed Richard Smith spotted one of the beasts swimming menacingly near his home in Reading.

'I was cycling on my own and I saw what I thought was a bough of a tree with four stubby branches on it close in to the bank,' gasped Richard. 'As I got closer I saw it was a crocodile. It was about four foot [1.2m] long. It had a two-foot tail and two-foot body. I got off my bike and ran back to where it was, but it had gone. I ran along the river for about 50 yards, but it wasn't there any more.'

Blimey O'Riley. The news of the sighting was the catalyst for more people to come forward with tales of terror and although the naturalists continued to insist that crocodiles, or indeed alligators, could not survive in the river's chilly waters, speculation about a killer in the Thames reached fever pitch. 'I think it is people letting their imaginations run away with them,' said crocodile expert Shaun Foggett, somewhat patronisingly.

A few days later Richard was vindicated – although not exactly in the way he might have expected. Richard *had* seen a crocodile but bizarrely it turned out to be a prop from a James Bond film rather than a real life man-eater. Improbable but true. The fake croc had been created for the 1973 film *Live and Let Die* with Roger Moore, specifically for the scene where 007 escapes the clutches of the baddies by running along the backs of a row of crocodiles – realism in that Bond era evidently wasn't high on Cubby Broccoli's agenda.

A chap by the name of Peter Wallace worked on the film as a boat consultant (remember the bit where the speedboat does an incredible 360-degree spin in midair?) and presumably helped himself to the prop as a souvenir when filming finished. He brought it back to England and stored it on an island on the Thames near Reading from where, we assume, it was washed into the river by flood water.

Thankfully Wallace's little memento from the set of *The Creature from the Black Lagoon* never found its way into the water.

FILM CREW'S
FAUX PAS
2013

The *X-Factor* is a television monster, the jewel in ITV's Saturday night schedule and damning proof that caterwauling, ritualised humiliation and Dermot O'Leary now appear to pass as family entertainment.

The show burst/flopped (delete according to personal preference) onto our screens in 2004 and ever since tens of thousands of excited/deluded (same again) hopefuls have turned up each year for the first round of auditions and the opportunity to pursue their dreams of fame/give everyone a chance to have a good laugh (one more time, please).

Over 8,000 wannabes trooped down to the ExCel Centre at the Royal Victoria Dock for the London leg of auditions in April 2013. The excitement was palpable and, in an innovative move, the show's producers decided to fly a state-of-the art helicam over the assembled hordes and get some lovely panoramic shots as they queued up like lambs to the slaughter.

Controlled remotely, the helicam was doing a fine job until gremlins found their inexorable way into the works and the pilot began to lose control. The chopper was in serious danger of crashing into the crowd and the pilot decided to ditch into the Thames rather than risk decapitating the next Leona Lewis or Olly Murs.

Sadly the footage from the helicam was successfully recovered after *X-Factor* bosses despatched a scuba diver to retrieve the AWOL drone.

'There was no way we could let a piece of kit like that just float down the Thames for anyone to find,' said a spokesperson.

The footage is stored inside the helicam so wouldn't have been damaged by the water. That meant anyone could have got their hands on it and seen everything we have filmed throughout the day.

Apart from not wanting anyone to see what we've got, we also would have lost vital scenes. The cameraman did the right thing crashing it into the river to avoid the fans on the ground but it was all a bit of a palaver. Thankfully no one was hurt and we managed to get a diver to fish the camera out of the river.

An aquatic rescue operation, it could be argued, on a cultural par with the raising of the *Mary Rose* or the restoration of the *Cutty Sark*.

SONNING'S FIRST-CLASS DELIVERY

2013

It was the English writer Jerome K. Jerome who, in his famous book *Three Men in a Boat*, described the little Berkshire Thames-side village of Sonning as 'the most fairy-like little nook on the whole river'. The celebrity likes of dramatist Sir Terrence Rattigan, football mentalist Glenn Hoddle and Led Zeppelin's Jimmy Page have all been residents at one time or another since then, but Sonning remained most renowned for the impression it made on Jerome in the late 19th century.

That all changed in September 2013, however, when the village unexpectedly and rather reluctantly became the focus of a bizarre Thames mystery, a story that spread around the world like wild fire.

What got tongues wagging and saw scores of reporters descend on Sonning was the sudden appearance of a new Royal Mail postbox in the village. It wasn't, of course, just any old postbox, oh no, this postbox had mysteriously been built into one of the buttresses of the village's brick bridge over the Thames. At just over a metre above the water line and around 10 metres (30ft) from the bank, the box could only be reached by boat and was, everyone agreed, about as useful as a Coalition Government.

Who the hell had installed it? Suspicion quickly fell on an idiotic Royal Mail employee, perhaps disorientated by sniffing the glue on all those stamps, but the company flatly denied any involvement. 'The recent appearance of a post box frontage on the side of the river bridge at Sonning is a mystery to us,' said a spokeswoman. 'It is certainly not an operational posting facility and we have no knowledge of how it arrived at this location.'

As the mystery deepened, so the theories to explain it became weirder. 'This is a very unusual village,' said long-term Sonning resident and acclaimed spoon-bender Uri Geller. 'I have never seen anything like this anywhere in the world. It's a new one on me. There are many sightings of a child ghost that walks on the bridge. Maybe it was the ghost of a mischievous little girl.'

Yep, Uri, it was a spectral toddler with a big chisel, cement mixer and obtuse sense of humour.

Sonning – and those eagerly following the story online around the world – waited with bated breath for someone to come forward and take responsibility but silence reigned. At the time of going to press, the elusive prankster had yet to be unmasked.

FLOOD FISHING
2014

Feel-good stories were in desperately short supply when the Thames flooded in early 2014 and with the news dominated by images of beleaguered residents abandoning their beloved homes, it was a harrowing period in the river's history.

Yet every cloud has a silver lining. In this case the lining was actually gold and it was in the deluged Surrey town of Egham in February that we finally had a flood tale to warm the heart rather than further dampen sodden spirits.

The hero of our story is Dave Pope, who was minding his own business on a street in the watery town when his eye was caught by something incongruous. Unsurprisingly, it was not a representative from the Environment Agency.

"I was walking down the road and suddenly saw a splash of orange," Dave explained. "I thought 'Ello ello', a goldfish. So I managed to catch him in my hands and put him in a teapot."

The work of our fishy saviour was not yet over. He quickly noticed two more confused refugees swimming in the waters of the Thames and after a mad dash for reinforcements, he successfully plucked both to safety.

"I rushed home to find another teapot and then my neighbour's children found a third one," Dave said. "I then transferred all three to a bucket. Hopefully I'll find the owner but failing that I'll give them to my brother to put them in his pond."

Dave quite rightly became a bit of a local celebrity after his heroics (despite his wife's dark mutterings about having to fork out for two new teapots) but our trio of rescued goldfish were not Egham's only tale of amazing animal escapology during the flood.

It was the day after the news of Dave's deeds broke. Egham was, ahem, awash with reporters covering the ongoing flooding and after doing his bit in front of camera, ITV's Simon Harris spotted a sweet wrapper floating past. Atop of the bag was a snail, who had evidently avoided a watery grave by climbing on board the improvised life raft and was now sailing serenely towards safety.

Quick-thinking Simon snapped the snail to prove he hadn't been enjoying a liquid lunch and although the eventual fate of our inventive gastropod is unknown, it's probably safe to assume it was the fastest it had ever travelled.

BIBLIOGRAPHY
BOOKS

The River Thames, Derry Brabbs, Frances Lincoln, 2010

I Never Knew That about the River Thames, Christopher Winn, Ebury Press, 2010

Eyots and Aits: Islands of the River Thames, Miranda Vickers, The History Press Ltd, 2012

The Thames: A Photographic Journey from Source to Sea, Derek Pratt, Adlard Coles Nautical, 2008

Bridges over the Thames, Ruth Mindell & Jonathan Mindell, Littlehampton Book Services Ltd, 1985

Liquid History: The Thames Through Time, Stephen Croad, Batsford Ltd, 2003

River Thames Book, Chris Cove-Smith, Imray, Laurie, Norie & Wilson Ltd, 2012

The Ghost Map: The Story of London's Deadliest Epidemic, Steven Johnson, Riverhead Books, 2006

Walks along the Thames Path, Ron Emmons, New Holland Publishers Ltd, 2001

Disasters on the Thames, Michael Foley, The History Press Ltd, 2011

WEBSITES

http://londonist.com
www.berkshirehistory.com
www.information-britain.co.uk
www.oxfordreference.com
www.historyofwar.org
www.bbc.co.uk/history
www.historyextra.com
www.britannia.com/history
www.portcities.org.uk
www.dailymail.co.uk
www.londononline.co.uk
www.thamesriverstrust.org.uk/facts-and-figures

www.riverthamesnews.com
www.forteantimes.com
www.mysteriousbritain.co.uk
http://theboatrace.org
www.british-history.ac.uk
www.hidden-london.com
www.museumoflondon.org.uk
www.thamespathway.com
www.projectbritain.com
www.hlf.org.uk
www.riverthamessociety.org.uk
www.secret-london.co.uk
www.visitthames.co.uk

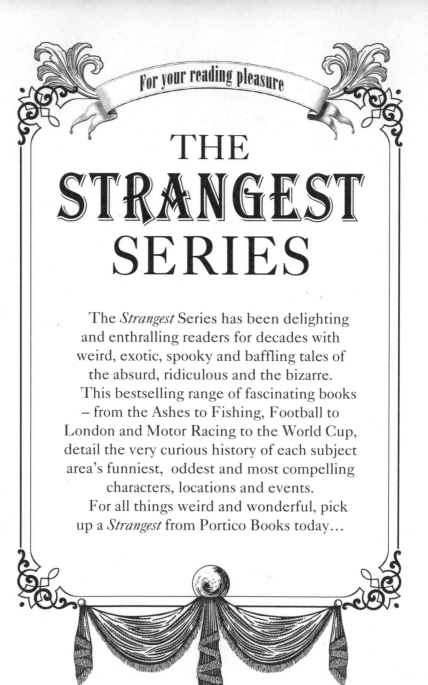

For your reading pleasure

THE
STRANGEST
SERIES

The *Strangest* Series has been delighting
and enthralling readers for decades with
weird, exotic, spooky and baffling tales of
the absurd, ridiculous and the bizarre.
This bestselling range of fascinating books
– from the Ashes to Fishing, Football to
London and Motor Racing to the World Cup,
detail the very curious history of each subject
area's funniest, oddest and most compelling
characters, locations and events.
For all things weird and wonderful, pick
up a *Strangest* from Portico Books today…